Praise for *Loveability:*
to Dating a

'Finally, an empowering advice book for teenage
girls. Brilliant and about time. Should be
compulsory reading.'
Mia Freedman,
founder/publisher Mamamia.com.au

'Without shaming or lecturing, and with plenty of wit
and warmth, *Loveability* will help girls carve their
own path through the thicket of mixed messages and
conflicting advice our culture gives them about love,
dating and relationships.'
Emily Maguire, author of
Your Skirt's Too Short: Sex, Power, Choice

'Possibly the first book in the world to treat
teenage girls as the responsible, intelligent human
beings they (mostly) are.'
Jane Caro, author, lecturer and
social commentator

Dannielle Miller (left) is co-founder and CEO of Enlighten Education, Australia's largest provider of in-school workshops for teen girls on body image, self-esteem and empowerment. She wrote a book for teen girls on how to claim their real power, *The Girl with the Butterfly Tattoo*, and a book for parents, *The Butterfly Effect: A Positive New Approach to Raising Happy, Confident Teen Girls*. She is also the parenting and women's issues expert for Channel 9's *Mornings*. Danni won an Australian Leadership Award (2011), was named Australia's number one Emerging Leader in Learning (2009) and was listed among Sydney's Top 100 Influential People by *The Sydney Morning Herald*'s magazine. She was NSW Entrepreneur of the Year (2007).

Nina Funnell (right) writes regularly on cultural and gender issues and her work has featured in places such as *The Sydney Morning Herald*, *The Age*, *The Australian* and *The National Times*. She has served as a member of the NSW Premier's Council on Preventing Violence Against Women, the National Children's and

Youth Law Centre board, and the expert advisory committee to the NSW Commission for Children and Young People. In 2010 Nina was awarded the Australian Human Rights Commission Community (Individual) Award and was a finalist for Young Australian of the Year for her advocacy work in sexual violence prevention.

Loveability

An Empowered Girl's Guide to Dating and Relationships

Dannielle Miller & Nina Funnell

Angus&Robertson
An imprint of HarperCollins*Publishers*

Angus&Robertson
An imprint of HarperCollins*Publishers*, Australia

First published in Australia in 2014
by HarperCollins*Publishers* Australia Pty Limited
ABN 36 009 913 517
harpercollins.com.au

Copyright © Nina Funnell and Dannielle Miller 2014

The rights of Nina Funnell and Dannielle Miller to be identified
as the authors of this work have been asserted by them under the
Copyright Amendment (Moral Rights) Act 2000.

This work is copyright. Apart from any use as permitted under the
Copyright Act 1968, no part may be reproduced, copied, scanned, stored
in a retrieval system, recorded, or transmitted, in any form or by any
means, without the prior written permission of the publisher.

HarperCollins*Publishers*
Level 13, 201 Elizabeth Street, Sydney NSW 2000, Australia
Unit D, 63 Apollo Drive, Rosedale, Auckland 0632, New Zealand
A 53, Sector 57, Noida, UP, India
1 London Bridge Street, London SE1 9GF, United Kingdom
2 Bloor Street East, 20th floor, Toronto, Ontario M4W 1A8, Canada
195 Broadway, New York NY 10007, USA

National Library of Australia Cataloguing-in-Publication data:

Miller, Dannielle, author.
  Loveability : an empowered girl's guide to dating and relationships /
  Dannielle Miller and Nina Funnell.
  ISBN: 978 0 7322 9646 9 (paperback)
  ISBN: 978 1 7430 9835 6 (ebook)
  Teenage girls—Life skills guides.
  Teenage girls—Conduct of life—Handbooks, manuals, etc.
  Friendship in adolescence.
  Social interaction in adolescence.
  Dating (Social customs).
  Funnell, Nina, author.
646.7608352

Cover design by Hazel Lam, HarperCollins Design Studio
Cover images by shutterstock.com
Typeset in 10.5/15pt Sabon LT Std by Kirby Jones

CONTENTS

Introduction   1

Chapter 1   Planet Romance — what to pack   7
Chapter 2   The loveability myth: pretty and
            hot = loveable   31
Chapter 3   Crushing dilemmas: what happens
            when the feelings are not mutual?   43
Chapter 4   Deal makers and deal breakers   61
Chapter 5   So you're dating! Now what?   81
Chapter 6   Your body, your rules: sex, power
            and consent   99
Chapter 7   Healing heartbreak   129
Chapter 8   Single? In a relationship? Who cares?
            I'm awesome!   165
Chapter 9   Relationship Q&A   197

Resources   243
Endnotes   253
Acknowledgments   257

INTRODUCTION

When you picked up this book, you probably expected to get all the answers from women who must have this whole relationship thing down to a fine art, right?

If that's what you're hoping for, then lady, unhand the book and walk away slowly ...

We are not those kinds of experts. Sure, we have formal expertise and qualifications (which you totally should check out at the front of the book, because it's always a good idea to suss out whom you're accepting advice from). But, really, we see ourselves more as tour guides. Think of this book as being like a travel guide to relationships. We will tell you about our travels, what we liked, what we hated, the places we would definitely go again and those you need to avoid ... and we will be asking other travellers to share their experiences, too.

So why did we decide to write this book?

One day we met for coffee and cake (as you do) and found ourselves browsing through the self-help section at a local bookshop. First we picked up a book called *The Catch: How to Be Found by the Man of Your Dreams*. Nina started squirming: 'How to be *found*? Why be so passive?'

Then Danni picked up *The Rules*, a highly successful book that promises that if a woman follows set guidelines that basically force her to act submissive and suppress her natural instincts, she will land a man. 'What?! This is insanity! How come we always need to change for him?' Danni asked. Oh, there was much eye rolling.

And these books are by no means isolated examples. There is a whole genre of books out there that would have young women believe that in order to attract love, they must be less of who they really are. Worse still, because these books are obsessed with proposals, the focus is all on the *ring*, but not the actual *relationship*.

A quick search online dished up the following gems for the gals: *How to Get Married in Less than a Year: Make Him Put a Ring on It in 365 Days or Less*; *Marry Him: The Case for Settling for Mr Good Enough*; *Why You're Not Married ... Yet: The Straight Talk You Need to Get the Relationship You Deserve*; *Why Men Marry Bitches: A Woman's Guide to Winning Her Man's Heart*; *Getting to 'I Do': The Secret to Doing Relationships Right*; and *Get Serious about Getting Married: 365 Proven Ways to Find Love in Less than a Year*.

Meanwhile the guys are reading: *Bang: More Lays in 60 Days*; *The Layguide: How to Seduce Women More Beautiful than You Ever Dreamed Possible No Matter What You Look Like or How Much You Make*; *How to Get the Girl: Ignore and Score!*; *How to Seduce a Woman and Get Her Sexually Addicted to*

You in 5 Steps; and the ever-so-subtle *Get Laid Now! How to Pick Up Women and Have Casual Sex.*

Spot the difference?

So we sat. And ate cake. There didn't seem to be any books at all that were offering the kind of advice we actually wanted when we were teen girls, such as how to survive crushes, tell if someone likes you, resolve fights, cope with heartbreak, know when it's time to break up and even (shock-horror!) enjoy being single (which can be awesome).

And while hundreds of studies are conducted on teenagers and sex every year, there are very few about teen *relationships*. In part, this is because teen relationships are often viewed as unworthy of academic research. But the reality is teen relationships are far from trivial. These early experiences help shape us and lay the foundation for our future relationships.

Then we launched into storytelling mode. Trading tales back and forth. The boys who were sweet but just not right for us. The times when we were devastated by the end of a relationship. And then there were the boys who made our hearts sing. The ones who made us laugh so hard we blew snot bubbles and/or snorted (which could be embarrassing but with the right boy only adds extra hilarity).

Oh, between us we had a wealth of travel tales.

So we decided that if none of the books out there already were particularly helpful, we should offer something different.

When we started talking about what we wanted the book to include, it became clear that each of us had expertise and experiences that made some chapters a more natural fit than others. So we decided that we'd write our own separate contributions rather than write each chapter together. (And let's be honest, we would never get anything done if we wrote together — can you imagine the talk and cake requirements?)

For you, it will be a little like hearing two quite separate voices, each with its own distinct personality ... and isn't that what we look for in real life when we need advice, anyway? Don't we go to one friend for advice on a particular topic, and another for a chat on a different issue?

And you're not going to hear just from us. Many of the teen girls Danni has connected with through her work with Enlighten Education have been honest and brave enough to pass on their thoughts — which, we might add, are incredibly warm and wise. We have also asked some very interesting, intelligent, feisty and fun women (some of whom also happen to be our friends — our posse rocks) to share their stories, too.

So you're in good hands. Multiple pairs of good hands, in fact.

Along the way we offer quizzes, as these can be a fun way to clarify your thoughts. And at the end of each chapter, we also offer affirmations. These are short, positive statements you can use to boost your strength or chart a new course in your life. Some people find it helpful to repeat an affirmation when they wake each morning, others when the going gets tough. Some like to write affirmations down and pin them up around the house. One mum sent Danni a picture of her bathroom mirror, where she and her daughter write affirmations each week so they are reminded to say them whenever they look at themselves. How cool is that?

Just so you know upfront, this book does not cover the physical practicalities of sex — the whole 'the penis goes in the vagina and babies are made' stuff. We feel that there are a lot of great books out there on this already (we list some of our faves in the back of the book) and we suspect that you have probably covered the nuts and bolts of reproduction at school. Instead we're going to talk about how to navigate relationships, sexuality, dating and feelings — which, when you think about it, are much more complex and equally, if not more, interesting and exciting.

Finally, we want to add that relationships come in all sorts of different shapes and sizes: that's how wonderful and diverse our hearts' desires are. Because some girls crush on boys, some girls crush on girls, and some girls crush on both, we've tried to use gender-neutral terms like 'partner', 'date' or 'crush' wherever possible. And if you want more information on gender or sexuality, we've also included some great resources at the back of the book.

So sit back, relax, strap on your seatbelt and let's get started!

CHAPTER 1

Planet Romance — what to pack

by Danni

If you're reading this book, there's a fair chance you want to develop a strong, healthy relationship. In this chapter I'll give you the basics — some pointers on how to get things started in the dating world.

Because I think you already have so much to offer, my job in this chapter is eassssy. All I need to do is offer you some pointers about communication skills to help you feel reassured that you've got this covered (I bet you will be nodding along furiously in agreement at these), convince you of your worth (again, eassssy with multiple s's — you are priceless) and then stand back and let you go!

Along the way I want to debunk some of the more unhelpful things you may hear about dating, just to make sure you don't get led down any dead-end streets on your journey to Planet Romance. Who needs misguided and misinformed advice at a time like this?!

The romance police

Most of us begin our trip to Planet Romance with crushes. Did you know that the intense emotions of a crush actually have their origins in a physical reality? Because the frontal lobes of your brain are still developing throughout your teens, you are all tuned up for emotions, fighting, running away and romance. Sound about right?

I really empathise with how very real and raw crush emotions are. In fact, I think I should win the Mother of the Year Award because I managed to get my daughter, Teyah, onto Channel 9's *Today* show set when her ultimate boy-band crushes were being interviewed. They walked right past us in the corridor, and Teyah was so overwhelmed that all she could do was sob. I helpfully yelled out, 'Welcome to Australia, guys — my daughter loves you!'

Sometimes our crushes are far more personal and we don't want the world to know about them. And when your crush happens to be a real-life-accessible human being (as opposed to a flying-around-the-world rock god) it can be confusing to know what to do, can't it? I mean, you aren't going to want your mum to step in at the canteen line at school and say, 'Hey! Welcome to the playground! My daughter loves you!'

Magazines are filled with advice on how to turn a crush into a relationship. Seriously, you'd think we should all be experts by the time we start dating. The titles often scream at us to curb our natural responses: '10 things he never wants to hear you say', 'How to play it cool with your crush', '20 things you shouldn't say to him'. It's interesting, isn't it, that so many magazines that claim to be written just for us seem to be mostly about him? I wonder how much better off we'd all be if we grew up on a diet of articles on how to make ourselves happy rather than a steady diet of articles about how to please boys (and about dieting — but that's a whole other story).

The magazine articles that claim to be able to show us how to connect with a crush often share a common message: if you really want to get The Man, you need to change your behaviour, stop following your instincts and follow certain rules.

The basic premise is that men like to hunt, so you need to play hard to get with a guy — for example, by not returning his call for at least two days after he first asks you out — in order to make him feel that you are in high demand and worth being hunted.

Crazily, girls are sometimes also told that they should play down their smarts, or act helpless so that guys get to feel good by coming to the rescue. I will admit some of the advice in these books and magazines can seem seductively sensible and helpful. But what good can really come from pretending you're *less* so that he can feel he's *more*? Ultimately, any advice that encourages us to follow particular commandments in order to win over a partner just doesn't sit well with me. Nor does any advice that asks girls to ignore their instincts in order to appear cool or unobtainable (see Chapter 6 to find out why this worries me so much).

And from a feminist perspective, telling girls to manipulate a situation just so boys will feel in charge is some major BS. What is it that the romance police are really saying? 'You're wonderful the way you are. But we will teach you how to be wonderful our way — which is a better kind of wonderful that boys will approve of more.'

Players, studs and stereotypes

Meanwhile, what are the boys reading? Magazines for young men — such as *FHM* and *ZOO Weekly* — seem preoccupied with showing breasts, discussing breasts, and even, in the case of *ZOO*, offering the chance to win your girlfriend new breasts. Yes, that's right, one year the magazine ran a competition in which one lucky reader won his girlfriend a boob job. Think sexual objectification with little or no emphasis on developing and nurturing relationships.

Boys receive the message that their masculinity is measured by whether they can score. And often they are told that in this particular game it's the guy who gets the hottest girl who wins.

> sexual objectification: treating a person as if they are only useful as a source of sexual pleasure for others

It's a message that was

popularised by Hugh Hefner, the *Playboy* founder known for surrounding himself with a bevy of young, surgically enhanced, scantily clad women. It's the same message advertisers peddle to guys: use a certain product and young, surgically enhanced, scantily clad women will be irresistibly drawn to you. This message has left a lot of boys feeling insecure, and a lot of girls angry about cultural double standards.

> double standard: when one person or group is treated differently from another person or group

The pressure on guys to hook up means that dating advice aimed at them is quite different to that for girls. A good example is the incredibly successful book *The Game: Penetrating the Secret Society of Pickup Artists*, which essentially teaches guys that it's OK to manipulate women and that learning new pick-up skills is no different to learning job interview skills. It gives tips on how a guy can speed up intimacy with a girl (sorry, I mean 'target') and how he can 'neg' her — that is, undermine her self-confidence with low-grade insults so she's more vulnerable to his advances. While we are dutifully following rules, they are being taught how to be players.

Assume, and you will make an 'ass' out of 'u' and 'me'

Let's take a moment to unpack what's happening on both sides of the fence in Relationship Advice World. It is assumed that girls are desperate for a relationship and must work hard to establish one, even if the guy may seem unwilling. And it is assumed that boys are only interested in one thing — sex — and that they need to work hard to get it, even if girls may seem unwilling.

Can you see how misleading, and potentially damaging, both views are, for girls and guys?

These assumptions encourage girls to have a defensive view of sexuality — that is, that they must be forever on the alert to stop boys' advances. It doesn't recognise that some girls are just as interested in exploring their sexuality, without being in a committed relationship, as some boys are.

Here is a powerful alternative viewpoint that might have you rethinking the popular assumptions about guys, too: research revealed that 75 per cent of guys would rather meet a girl they liked enough to date than just casually hook up.[1] It also highlighted just how similar boys' goals are to many girls'. Boys' reasons for dating included:

- **Companionship and connection.** Boys genuinely like the girls they date and want to spend more time with them.
- **Emotional support and intimacy.** Boys like having someone to talk to and feel supported by.
- **Physical intimacy.** This was offered as a secondary reason to date. Most boys see

sexual intimacy as a result of dating, not the reason to date.
- **Peer groups.** Some boys date so they don't feel left out by their friends who are paired up.

Boys saw one of the big downsides to dating as being the risk of rejection — of having a broken heart.

It seems, too, that despite what popular culture tells us about teen guys only chasing the 'hotties', most young men actually look for a partner who is 'funny, nice, outgoing, understanding of others, able to make decisions and reasonably self-confident'.

Ground-breaking news, girls: guys are just as likely to want a meaningful relationship as we are, and are looking for similar qualities in a partner to those that we value. Why, then, do any of us need silly games? And why should girls leave taking the initiative and establishing the relationship guidelines up to boys?

Research shows that boys tend to be at least two years behind girls in terms of emotional maturity during the teen years, so they are often less able than girls to articulate their feelings or know how to develop relationships with girls. If a girl is more relationship savvy and more emotionally intelligent than her boy crush, she may well be better placed to take the lead.

> Many teenagers and young adults still expect guys to 'wear the pants' in the relationship and be in

charge. Yet girls are generally considered to be the relationship experts, which means the non-expert is in charge. That doesn't sound like a good plan to me.
Andrew P. Smiler[2]

Rules schmooles

So if the dating advice we get from books, magazines, movies and TV shows is at best not particularly helpful, and at worst makes things more difficult between boys and girls, how did it get so popular?

People tend to prefer information or research that supports the beliefs they already have. (Psychologists call this 'confirmation bias'.) Let's say you read a guide to boys that tells you they don't like girls who appear too keen and that you really must wait at least two days before returning a guy's messages. This may sound really accurate to you as you recall all the times when a guy you liked (or a friend liked) seemed keen, then when the enthusiasm was returned immediately, he withdrew.

But let's get real. Nearly all the really great couples I know say that when they first met, it was obvious there was an attraction and that both parties couldn't get enough of each other from the word go. There are many successful couples in which the girl made it known almost immediately that she was very into him, and he loved that.

I went up to him and I said, 'Hey, I think you're cute. Can I have your number?' He said yes and we ended up dating for about ten months. It was a good ten months, because we had been honest from the start, [so] neither of us had to pretend and [we] felt comfortable from the start! I say who cares about the rules, do what you feel is right.

Yaminah, 17

I met my boyfriend, who I have been with now for a year, at school. As soon as I saw him I just walked over and said hello and asked for his number, and then I called him after school and said, 'Hey, it's the crazy girl from school and I really like you — do you like me?' He said yes and then I said, 'So what are we going to do about it?' and he asked me out.

Mikayla, 14

Well, we were friends for a month before things became 'official' and we were both really affectionate, so I knew I had nothing to be scared of. I sat down with him one night and told him that I really, really felt for him. He said he was glad I did this because he was nervous about how I was going to react if he told me first!

Bryanna, 15

I want to be clear here. I am not advocating that you need to now become the 'huntress'. Then we'd just be back to square one, only this time you'd be the one convinced you need to do the chasing and look for suitable prey. It's *not* a jungle out there!

Rather, what I am saying is that you are probably already well equipped to be all the things guys say they like in a partner: 'funny, nice, outgoing, understanding of others, able to make decisions and reasonably self-confident'.

The real communication dos and don'ts

> My version of flirting is looking at someone I find attractive multiple times and hoping they are braver than I am.
> **Internet meme**

This meme makes me giggle, for I think it sums up how intimidating talking to your crush can seem. You'll be reassured to know it needn't feel so overwhelming.

In this section I want to offer you some basic communication guidelines that will help improve your interactions with someone you're interested in. But here's the really cool thing: these guidelines are universal and will help improve your interactions with everyone you meet — new friends of either sex, teachers, your parents. The ability to communicate effectively is one of the most valued employability skills you will ever develop, too. I love the idea that these guidelines will not only make you feel more equipped for your heart's work but also prepare you for your head's work, your career.

1. Figure out whom you want to be in a relationship with and why.

You're thinking this part is easy, right? That one — the cute one!

But there really is more to it than that. To form a relationship with someone, you need to first learn more about you rather than more about them — how refreshing! You need to know what your values are and what you want from a relationship. This activity should help:

- Get a big blank piece of paper and write across the top: 'What values are important to me in a relationship?'
- Start making a list. There are no right or wrong answers, simply values that matter to you in a relationship — such as freedom, trust and honesty. It's not about what matters to your best friend, parents or teachers. This is *your* list.
- When you hit a pause, ask yourself, 'What else is important to me in a relationship?' and keep going.

- Once you feel that you've come up with everything you can think of, read your list and edit it. There might be some things that, upon reflection, you decide aren't that important to you, or some that are similar and can be combined.
- Now it's time to rank them. Give each value a number, starting at number one for the most important. If you find it difficult to rank them, ask yourself, 'If I could have *only one* of these qualities in my relationship, which one would it be?' Then keep working through the list until each one has a number.
- Look at your top five values. You will be genuinely happy if your top five are present in your relationship most (if not all) of the time. The other ones on the list are important, too, but are not as essential to your happiness.

If you're in a relationship and feel that it's not quite working for you, doing this exercise can be a good way to clarify if your most important needs are being met — and if they're not, then you can find ways to do something about that. Your values will change as you get older. For example, now you might feel that it's really important to have freedom in a relationship, so you can explore and develop your tastes in what you like, but later, security might become more important to you. Check in with yourself every so often to see whether your values have changed, so you can continue to get the most out of your relationships. You can adapt this activity to trying to decide what qualities you value in a friend or what type of job you might enjoy the most.[3]

2. Get involved in a range of activities.
Many girls tell me their biggest problem is not being able to meet a partner they like. My advice is: get involved, sista! Join a drama club, Venturers, a local youth group or a mixed sporting team. By doing something you enjoy, you are far more likely to meet someone who has similar interests to you, too, aren't you?

3. Introduce yourself and remember names.
The basics matter. Just walk on over and say hi and give your name, with a big friendly smile. This is really an essential skill for life. I know that whenever a young person bothers to make eye contact with me and introduce herself, I remember her. Your crush is no different! Don't just be 'the chick from maths', be *you*.

4. Work on your conversation skills so you get better at listening and talking.
I think it's important that not all your communication is done via text or Facebook, particularly in the early getting-to-know-each-other phase. I can tell you from first-hand experience that even if you have great

chemistry with a guy via email or messaging, in real life things may not flow quite so easily. If you develop a closeness online and it doesn't translate into real life, you'll both feel really uncomfortable and also, perhaps, a little sad that you shared so much of yourself with someone that you know you'll never really connect with long term. And girls crushing on gamers who are most at home behind their computer screens may need to encourage them to talk for reals, not just via messaging.

Great conversationalists tend to do the following:

- Ask questions. When someone asks questions, it shows they are interested in the other person and his or her opinion. Open questions — ones that require more than a mere yes or no — really help get the conversation flowing. For example, try 'Why did you pick basketball as a sport?' rather than 'So, do you like basketball?'
- Offer observations or examples to show they understand or empathise with what the other person is saying. An example is 'Yep, I felt like that, too, when I started at this school. It can be so lonely being the newbie. How did you cope?' (See how I also threw in an open-ended question there? Genius.)
- Show they are listening by referring back to what the other person has said, in a meaningful way and making connections

where possible. An example is 'Wow, *The Catcher in the Rye* is my favourite book, too! What part do you love the most?' (PS That is my favourite book; I could chat about it all day! If we ever meet, you should totally ask me about it.)

And in any real-world interaction, it's not just about what people say to each other, but also about what their bodies are saying. The following body-language cues indicate a person is interested in you and what you're saying. They act as your 'green light' to continue, safe in the knowledge that someone is engaged with what you're saying.

- **Posture.** They look comfortable, and they are perhaps leaning in close to you or, occasionally, touching you. Their arms aren't crossed. They seem relaxed.
- **Eye contact.** Looking into the other person's eyes, particularly when they are speaking, indicates interest in that person. I love to look into people's eyes when they are speaking to me, as I get a real insight into how they are truly feeling. They say the eyes are the window to the soul, and I so agree.
- **Nodding in agreement.** When someone nods in response to key things you're saying, they're showing interest and understanding.

- **Smiling or laughing.** A smile or laughter is a very strong indication that the person is enjoying what you're saying. They are body-language 'gold stars'.

Keep these body-language basics in mind when you are listening, too. If you like what you're hearing, show it.

Now for the negatives ...

Negative body language isn't necessarily a red light indicating the person you are speaking to has completely lost interest. The signals listed below may also indicate that a person is tired, preoccupied with other thoughts or nervous. However, it is important to be aware of these signs, as they will help you gauge whether the other person is right there with you:

- **Appearing tense or nervous.** Signs that indicate someone might not be interested include frowning, crossing arms, fidgeting and looking around you as if for someone else to talk to.
- **Yawning.** They've either had a late night, or you're losing them. (Note to self: if someone is talking to you and you can't stop yawning, but you really are enjoying what they're saying, it's a good idea to apologise and explain that you are interested, you are just tired.)

Some girls are very social and love talking to new people, but for others, social occasions can be trying.

Michaela, one of Enlighten Education's Facebook friends, stands in front of groups of strangers and talks every day for her job, but she was 'cripplingly shy' when she was a girl. Her advice is to start small:

You can eat an elephant if you take small enough bites, right? So think about one thing you'd like to work on that challenges you in social settings, and give yourself one small goal. For example, maybe think about saying hello to just one person you've not met before. If you manage it, that's great! Just one hello. Then build from there ... The more you do it, the easier it gets.

Wise advice. Start small and practise. Every smile that is returned or conversation that lasts more than five minutes will help build your confidence.

5. Be sensitive to other people.
Your crush may be feeling nervous, too. Look for body-language clues to help you gauge that, and offer lots of supporting comments — like 'That's great!' or 'Wow, that's interesting, tell me more' — or at the very least flash some smiles for encouragement.

6. Take compliments and give them sincerely.
I am always disappointed when I see people reject compliments. And I see girls do this a lot. You've probably noticed this kind of thing, too: a girl posts a

gorgeous photo of herself on Facebook and when one of her friends takes the time to write a lovely comment such as 'You're so beautiful!' she writes back something like 'As if. You are.'

I think of compliments as being like little word-gifts someone has boxed up, tied with a ribbon and presented to another person. If someone handed you a sparkly present to unwrap, would you throw it back at them, or refuse to thank them for it?

I don't think girls reject or ignore compliments because they intend to be rude, but rather because they are so terrified that others will think they are 'up themselves'.

For a whole bunch of messed-up reasons, the ultimate sins we like to attack girls for are being fat, being a slut and thinking she's 'all that'. True? I recall once, when I was fighting with my bestie in Year 9, that she said to me, 'You are such a fat slut and you think you're so much better than everyone else.' Wow. The girl-hating trifecta!

But just as cruel words can scar us, kind words and compliments can have a profoundly positive, healing effect on us. I love the anecdotes some of my teen friends shared with me:

At a debating competition one time I was wearing different earrings, one a sparkly one, the other a green flower, and one of the guys on the other team came up to me at the end and said, 'I've been staring at you all night, your earrings are so quirky,' then

smiled and walked away. I was so happy for the rest of the night and I didn't even know the guy!
Erin, 14

I was at a friend's party, and the guy I was talking to found out that I was a Star Wars geek and he said, 'I think you may be the Obi Wan for me!' We laughed for ages and now we're really good friends.
Brinley, 15

I was talking to a friend about how I really enjoyed ancient history. He said he loved the ancient Greeks and started going into great detail about all the gods and goddesses, attempting to teach me all of them. After about twenty minutes he got to the 'last one', Aphrodite, and he said, 'Do you know who she is?' And I said, 'Yes, she's the goddess of beauty,' and he said, 'Yep, that's right, and you're the living embodiment of her.' Couldn't stop smiling after that.
Steph, 15

7. Be willing to risk rejection, because it is possible that someone you approach may not be interested.

I know. This is shocking news, isn't it? What's. Not. To. Love. About. You? Adopt the approach I take in business towards rejection: a no is not a no forever, it is just a no for that day. It's possible that the person who rejects you now may well be interested in you later on.

Or it's possible that the other person is great but just doesn't believe you are compatible, for whatever reason. That's OK. Not everyone likes Caramello Koalas, either, and that also makes little sense to me.

Or it's possible that this person is a jerk who shouldn't even be in your life.

Don't overthink it.

Quiz

Circle the answer that comes closest to describing your situation.

1. There's someone in your maths class you like. You:

- A. Do nothing about it as you're worried they will reject you.
- B. Start flirting up a storm with their best mate. They need to know you're hot property.
- C. Smile at them, ask how their weekend was and volunteer to help them out when they look confused about how to follow the rules of trigonometry (you totally rock at trig, BTW). Nothing may come from initiating a friendship, but at least you'll get to know them.

2. Someone you've had a crush on for ages asks you to the movies on Friday night. You:

- A. Say no. You're too shy around them and wouldn't know what to say.

Planet Romance — what to pack

- B. Tell them you've got other plans (even though you haven't) but might be free on Saturday (it's best to keep them eager).
- C. Tell them you'd love to. If you feel nervous, you suggest going with a group of friends, which will take the pressure off you both.

3. Someone from school you are crushing on sends you a cute-and-flirty text message. You:

- A. Ignore it. You're not sure what to say back and you're worried they're just joking.
- B. Start sending them loads of flirty messages, too.
- C. Send them a cute-and-flirty message back, then at school smile and tell them their text was sweet. You don't want to get caught up in an only-online flirt fest. If you're going to have a real relationship, you'd like to know sooner rather than later and be in a position where you can read their body language, too.

4. Someone you like sends you a Facebook message that you really don't understand. You:

- A. Assume it means they don't like you or are making fun of you.
- B. Analyse it to death, ask all your friends what it means and stare at it for hours hoping to break the code.
- C. Tell them you didn't get it and ask them to explain.

5. You have heard that your crush likes you but is too shy to say hello. You:

   A. Assume that they mustn't like you at all. If they did, they'd make the first move.
   B. Smile and hope that they will build up the courage to speak to you eventually.
   C. Break the ice by asking them about a singer you know they're really interested in. You feel shy, too, but you know that this is the only way to really find out if there is any chemistry between you both.

6. Someone you like asks you out but then needs to cancel at the last minute, which really disappoints you. You:

   A. Refuse to even listen to their reasons why they had to change the plans. They are obviously just not that into you.
   B. Pretend that you don't mind and tell them you will make sure you are free when it next suits them.
   C. Tell them you are disappointed but give them the opportunity to explain why they had to cancel. If their explanation sounds reasonable, you agree to catch up at another time that suits you both.

7. How often do you read articles in magazines that offer you 'dating rules' and 'flirting tips'?

   A. Constantly. You have no idea what you are doing!
   B. Constantly. You want to be the best at this dating game!

C. Sometimes. It can be helpful to get a variety of opinions on relationships, but ultimately you need to do what feels right for you.

Now add up how many A's, B's and C's you circled, and check below.

Mostly A's

Sweetheart, before you think too much more about loving *someone else*, you might need to spend a little more time learning how to love *you*. Sometimes we think we will feel better about ourselves if we find another who can heal us; this rarely works long term.

Mostly B's

Your beliefs around romance may have been influenced by popular culture and the media — and while there's nothing wrong with that, you might want to think about trusting your own inner voice more and letting others fall in love with the real you, not a version of you that you think they will like best.

Mostly C's

You've got a really sensible attitude towards dating and relationships. This doesn't mean you won't find elements of dating scary or bewildering — all new experiences can be. But with your solid sense of self and honest approach, you're bound to attract like-minded partners eventually.

Affirmations

I have a lot to offer in any relationship.

I value all of me and attract others who value all of me, too.

CHAPTER 2

The loveability myth: pretty and hot = loveable

by Danni

While all the advice in Chapter 1 will help you in the dating world, I know through my work with Enlighten Education that many girls often wonder about something far more fundamental than how to talk to, and relate to, their crushes: they question whether they are beautiful enough to be loved.

Girls sometimes make the mistake of thinking they need external validation that they have the look they believe will bring them love. This is why some girls are drawn to Facebook pages that rate them based on their looks, or feel compelled to ask people to 'like' their profile pictures.

This is also why so many girls believe that if they were models sashaying down the catwalk, they would finally know their worth — and that the boys would come running!

It's understandable if you feel this way. You are far from alone. A girl may have her own individual reasons for being uncomfortable about her appearance, but all girls and women share at least one thing: we are at war with our bodies because there is a war being waged on our bodies. We get messages about what makes us beautiful and worthy of love from TV, the internet, the music we listen to and videos we watch, magazines and the ads we see everywhere. We are constantly being told what we should look like, and the definition of beauty has become very narrow: it's all about being pretty, thin and hot.

But you know what? Girls who don't fit conventional notions of beauty and girls who do are equally likely to have successful relationships. We mustn't fall into the trap of trying to measure our loveability via the mirror or a set of scales.

Model obsession

One of my closest friends, Nikki Davis, works with me in schools empowering girls. Nikki also models and says the main reason she was drawn to modelling as a teen girl 'was the simple pleasure of having confirmation that I was special. It validates that you have the "right" look. You think breaking into modelling will cancel out any of your self-esteem issues and doubts because it means that you are what society thinks is beautiful and special. But of course the reality is far more complicated than that.

'Modelling can change the way both girls and guys see you. People sometimes make an immediate assumption that I'm not particularly bright, and that is incredibly frustrating. Guys might assume that all models are party girls and I must be out all night at bars. Or they only want to date you so they can show you off to their friends. (I am not a trophy!)

'And just because some guys may be more likely to approach me, it does not mean they are necessarily the right kind of guys for me or that they may actually want a relationship with me. It often seemed it was the most arrogant guys in a room who wanted to show off to their mates by chatting up a "model".

'Ultimately, in all my relationships, after a few months the novelty of my looks would wear off. We'd then be left with the essentials — whether we were actually compatible as people. We'd have the same issues all couples have — everything from how much time he would spend with mates to how much mess I left with my make-up in his bathroom. In fact, at times I felt like I was a particularly disappointing girlfriend to some guys as I perhaps didn't live up to their expectations of me as being "perfect". Just like any other girl, I have had my fair share of both rejection and affection.'

(Nikki is now happily married, to a very genuine man who loves all of her, even her mess-in-the-bathroom ways.)

When a teen girl looks at me and asks, 'Do you think I could be a model?' I know it's insane to try to answer the question factually. Ideas about what makes a girl attractive are subjective, and what the fashion industry finds attractive can be mystifying to us ordinary folk. Really, the only person who can answer the question is someone at a modelling agency. What I try to do is unpack the real questions that lie beneath it. 'Do you think I could be a model?' is not just a question about career choices. It's also shorthand for 'Do you think I'm beautiful? Do you think I'm special? Do you think I will be loved?' And the answer to that should be easy. All girls are beautiful. And special. And yes, you will be loved — I guarantee it.

Beauty myths: the bizarre, the dangerous, the controlling

Throughout history, women have tried all manner of odd techniques and rituals to boost their attractiveness and find a partner. But believe me, all the self-loathing we get caught up in and the extreme measures some of us go to in order to fit a narrow definition of beauty are not helpful, nor are they genuinely attractive.

Early Egyptian queen Cleopatra used crushed carmine beetles mixed with ground-up ant eggs as lipstick. In Japan, geishas and kabuki actors used nightingale droppings to remove the thick make-up from their faces. Venetian women achieved blonde highlights by pouring lion urine on their locks and then sitting out in the sun.

I bet you're amused and thinking about how odd such grooming rituals are. Once, when I was on my way home from a trip to New Zealand, I stopped to buy some duty-free and stumbled upon an equally bizarre beauty product: a face cream that boasts sheep's placenta as an ingredient.

I have now discovered that facial products and treatments containing placenta — and not just sheep's but *human* placenta, too — are apparently the ultimate in organic beauty.

Seriously, who would want to rub sheep's placenta on her face?

During the 1600s in Europe, fashionable beauties would paint their faces with a white lead powder in order to appear paler. (It caused their skin to rot.) In the nineteenth century, Englishwomen consumed the poison arsenic as it gave the skin an interesting glow. (It also, eventually, killed them.) Can you see a pattern here? Suffer for beauty even if it means leaving behind a hot corpse?

Today, too, we use some frightening-sounding things on our skin. Botox is a neurotoxin — a substance that interrupts nerve signals — produced by the bacterium *Clostridium botulinum.* It is incredibly toxic — for instance, it causes botulism, a very serious form of food poisoning — yet it can also be turned into a medical and cosmetic treatment. Because it interrupts messages between nerves and muscles, effectively paralysing the muscles, it creates a wrinkle-free effect in the area where it is injected. Botox injection is now the fastest growing cosmetic practice.

Sometimes beauty rituals have been less about trying to achieve a pretty face and more about enhancing a woman's desirability by limiting her personal power.

Foot binding was once very common in China, starting around 1000 AD. Up to 2 billion Chinese women — almost half of the female population — had their feet bound up until the practice was officially banned in 1912, although some women still did it in secret.

The custom involved breaking the toes on a young girl's foot and then tightly binding them underneath the sole of her foot with bandages. This practice would prevent the foot from growing and would ensure the girl's foot remained tiny.

Small feet were a sign of status and were necessary for a young woman to be judged desirable enough to marry into a wealthy family. Unsurprisingly, the practice was painful and led to complications such as the skin on the foot becoming putrid; in fact, it was not uncommon for one or more toes to drop off. Certainly the woman's mobility was then very limited — hobbling on shrunken feet, she was literally bound to her home and husband.

While it is easy to look at all these practices and giggle at how misguided they are, we, too, fall prey to myths around beauty and messages that would have us equate our looks with love.

How often have you or one of your friends worn really uncomfortable high heels and hobbled around all night in agony, telling yourself it is worth the pain because they look amazing?

And we, too, fall prey to wanting to bandage, and mutilate ...

Plastic girls

When I was a toddler, I was burnt; I have a very noticeable third-degree burn scar on my right arm.

As a self-conscious teen I would have given anything to rid myself of my scar, and I thought that because of it, no boy would love me. Now as a woman I realise our differences, our quirks and our scars are what make us unique. I have embraced my burn as part of my story and wear the tight, twisted flesh with a sense of pride. It is a visible reminder of my strength and endurance. And, just for the record, no guy I've ever been interested in has been in the least bit put off by it.

Yet increasingly I have noticed that the media and popular culture do not embrace diversity; our physical differences are presented as problems that need to be solved through medical intervention.

Many celebrities have the one generic, geometrically perfect face; they feature the same bee-stung lips, chiselled cheekbones, wide eyes and wrinkle-free brow. It is the look Hollywood equates with beauty and with those who will win the hearts of leading men. But plastic surgery and other cosmetic procedures are not solely for celebrities or accident victims; they are very much mainstream.

It is getting easier all the time to spot someone who has had 'work'. This is partly because more people are making the decision to have plastic surgery. There is another reason, too. People increasingly want their surgery to be identifiable. 'There is an [increase in] requests to look "done" rather than for me to create a more natural look,' facial cosmetic surgeon Dr William Mooney says. The move away from a natural look is particularly noticeable in the case of breast enhancements. Dr Mooney says, 'In Australia there has been an increase of between ten and fifteen per cent in the size of the implants being used over the course of the past five years,' says Dr Mooney. Basically, more people are beginning to see the ideal body as one that looks like it has been altered with plastic surgery.

Dr Mooney explained to me that many patients want cosmetic surgery as they believe their new look will bring them a relationship or a better job or increased happiness. 'The reality is, it won't,' he said. 'Patients who are looking for this are going to be disappointed. I like to explain that all surgery really can do is change the symmetry or the geometry [the proportions] of a face or body; it doesn't have any magical power. What makes us loveable is far more elusive and more difficult to measure.'

When we see ourselves and other girls and women as just bodies, we forget that we are all actually *somebodies*.

And that anyone worthy of being with you in a relationship will want to be with *all* of you — not just one of your body parts.

Quiz

**Circle the answer that comes closest
to describing your situation.**

1. Do you feel that you would have a lot to offer a potential partner?

- A. Not really. You don't think you are the kind of girl that other people find attractive.
- B. Yes. You always get hundreds of 'likes' on your Facebook profile pics.
- C. Yep. You are enough.

2. How often do you compare your body to those of girls in magazines to assess your loveability?

- A. Frequently. And you don't measure up.
- B. Frequently. And you can see that you have the look that will make guys fall for you.
- C. Not often. No good can come from playing the compare-and-despair game. And besides, the images are all fake, as they are Photoshopped.

3. How often do you fantasise about looking like the models you see on the covers of magazines?

- A. All the time.
- B. Sometimes.
- C. Rarely. You know you are enough.

4. When you look in the mirror, you:

A. Spend a lot of time picking out all your flaws and criticising yourself for them.
B. Notice some things about yourself that you would like to change.
C. Feel fine about what you see. After all, the image we see reflected has been distorted by society's perceptions of what defines beauty, anyway!*

I had stickers that say exactly this made for mirrors, and they're available in the Enlighten Education online shop. They're a great reminder not to get sucked into body-image angst!

5. If your crush asked you out, you would:

A. Begin dieting and worrying excessively about what you might wear.
B. Take ages to pick an outfit that you feel attractive in.
C. Feel excited and wear something you like that you know you will feel both happy and comfortable in.

6. When a friend or crush compliments your appearance, you usually say:

A. 'As if! You're the gorgeous one.' You know no-one could really find you attractive.
B. Say thanks but worry that perhaps the person wasn't being sincere.
C. Say thanks, smile and feel happy.

The loveability myth: pretty and hot = loveable

7. You bump into your crush at the shops just after you've finished netball and you're looking all sweaty and dishevelled. How do you feel?

- A. Devastated. There's no way your crush will like you now.
- B. Fine, because you run the other way so your crush won't see you. And you then swear you will never leave the house without being fully made-up again. Somebody pass the mascara!
- C. Fine. Your crush might as well see the real you — and at least they'll know you take your sport seriously.

Now add up how many A's, B's and C's you circled, and check below.

Mostly A's

Gorgeous girl, you mightn't be able to see it right now, but there is so much to love about you. When we get hung up on body anxiety, we tend to hide our whole unique, beautiful selves from the world. It's time to stop letting your concerns over how you look hold you back from making a real connection with others.

Mostly B's

It can be fun to spend time on your outfit and make-up, and to get compliments on your looks. Just don't forget that you are *so* much more than your body. When someone genuinely loves you, they'll love you when you're slouching around the house in uggs with no make-up on just as much as when you've spent ages in front of the mirror.

Mostly C's

Keep it up, sista! You see your worth not just in terms of your looks. You know that you are enough just the way you are and that you have a lot to offer in a relationship. Of course, there will still be ups and downs along the way — but stay true to yourself and you will be on the path to fulfilling relationships.

Affirmations

I choose to send loving thoughts to myself and others.

I embrace all of me, knowing that nobody is perfect.

CHAPTER 3

Crushing dilemmas: what happens when the feelings are not mutual?

by Nina

When I was in high school, I often felt as though I was destined to walk through life alone. I had plenty of guy friends and more than a few crushes, but as far as the dating game went, I was the eternal single-pringle. So while my friends were off with their boyfriends, I was busy flipping through relationship advice columns in teen-girl magazines, *imagining* what it would be like to have a boyfriend. And there was certainly no shortage of relationship columns to keep my imagination active.

What I remember most about those relationship articles are the pictures that went along with them. You know the ones I'm talking about. The Perfect Couple.

Kissing on the swings. Lying in a field. Embracing at sunset on a dock.

During the summer months, The Perfect Couple would be pictured sharing a giant slice of watermelon. He'd give her piggyback rides along the beach, and they'd draw love hearts with their initials in the sand. During the winter months, you'd find them sheltering in the rain or rugging up by a camp fire with hot cocoa.

On one level I knew that it was all a mirage, an optical illusion created by a team of stylists, hair and make-up artists, photographers and wardrobe assistants. I knew that in every image where the models were posed as if they were sharing an intimate, private moment, there was, in reality, a photographer standing a metre away, camera clicking furiously (talk about a mood killer!). And it never escaped me that the magazines weren't only selling romance: they were also selling products, such as the clothes the models were wearing.

Despite all this, these images still sold me on the fantasy that somewhere there were *real* couples that looked and acted this way. And I knew that I wasn't one of them. I was missing out.

Not that my single-pringle status ever stopped me from filling out quizzes intended for girls with boyfriends. (My imaginary boyfriend and I would always score top marks, by the way.) But all of this romance stuff left me feeling kind of ... hollow. Every article or quiz that presumed I had a boyfriend only served to highlight the fact that I didn't.

Fairy tales and romantic comedies didn't make my life any easier. When you think about it, our culture is practically obsessed with telling girls that unless you've got a man-bag on your arm, your life is not complete. No wonder we feel pressure. And no wonder so many girls feel like everyone else is dating except them. (By the way, this isn't even close to true. Being single is waaaay more common than most of us are led to believe. Just look around you and you will probably be surprised by how many fantastic single girls you know! And for more on the topic of how to rock being single, you should check out Chapter 8.)

I recently sat down and rewatched all the Disney fairy tales. I was struck by how quickly the women fall in love and get hitched. Sleeping Beauty and Cinderella sealed the deal after just one date. Snow White did one better, winning her prince's heart with just one song. Talk about speed dating.

In real life, it takes a little longer. We also tend to kiss a few frogs along the way. After surveying 2000 people, one study conducted by the dating site meeteez.com found the average female will have her heart broken five times and kiss an average of twenty-two frogs before finally meeting a good match![1] Another study found that the average number of relationships it takes to develop a good idea about what it is that you really want is twelve.[2]

This doesn't mean that you need to date twelve people (or kiss twenty-two) before you find someone you can click with. Nor is there just one person out there whom you will be compatible with. (This is great news, too, because can you imagine how long it would take to find that one sole soul mate?) So in this chapter we're going to talk about what happens when a crush doesn't follow the plot of a romcom or fairy tale. Specifically we're going to look at what happens when you like someone who just doesn't reciprocate your feelings, or what to do if someone has a crush on you and the feelings are not mutual. Both of these situations crop up regularly in dating land so it's good to get our bearings early. Whether you're in a relationship or are yet to start dating, this chapter will help you identify and navigate some of the common pitfalls associated with crushes.

Unrequited love

Oh yeah! Enjoy the hunt.

Picture this. You've met someone who is gorgeous, funny and smart. Just thinking about them makes you smile. Your crush is practically perfect in every single way. There's only one small problem. You're not actually dating. Maybe your crush is dating (or crushing on) someone else. Maybe they haven't really noticed you, or you haven't got to spend much time together. Or maybe your crush's band/sport/study is more important than you right now. Still, you're convinced that this is the perfect person for you, and once your stars align and the timing is correct, you will make the perfect couple, right?

Hello, Miss Unrequited Love. Sometimes these crushes do work out for the best. A friend of mine had a secret crush on a girl for years. One day while standing in the middle of a shopping centre, he got a text message alert from her. Ecstatic, he broke into his happy dance. He then opened the text and it said, 'Hey, I can see you.' He turned around and she was standing about twenty metres away and looking very amused. Luckily it turned out that she felt the same way, too, but had always been unsure of his feelings. And that is how the two of them got together. Cute, huh?

Of course it doesn't always work out that well. Sometimes we find ourselves longing for people who aren't available. It's a cliché, but when I was in Year 10 I spent a good six months crushing on a boy who was so obviously gay that apparently I was the only one who didn't know. Looking back, part of the reason I spent so many of my teen years as a singleton was because I was so busy crushing on unavailable guys, or guys who weren't that into me, that I didn't even notice the ones who *were* into me.

One thing even more confusing than unrequited love is meeting someone who is semi-interested and who semi-reciprocates your feelings. It often goes like this: you meet someone who gives you butterflies. You'd love for something to happen between the two of you, and to a certain extent they seem keen. Well, sort of. They'll hook up with you at parties, but they don't want to officially call you their girlfriend. They'll flirt outrageously in person, but don't ever bother to text or call you. You've probably met their friends (unless they're trying to keep you a secret, which is never a good sign, by the way), but they haven't made an effort to get to know your family or friends.

Fine, you think to yourself. I can be patient. Maybe they're afraid of commitment. Maybe they just need some time. The last person they dated was totally crazy (at least according to them), so you don't want to come across as needy or overly keen. Besides, they'll come around eventually, won't they?

Maybe. It has been known to happen in the history of dating — once or twice.

But here is something to keep in mind: if someone really, truly cares about you, not only will they tell you as much, they'll also *act* in a way that makes you *feel* cared for. And if they genuinely want to be with you, they'll be willing (even eager!) to *work* at being with you. By 'work' I mean making an effort to spend time with you, caring about your opinions and feelings, being willing to meet your friends and family and generally not wanting to date people who are not you.

So if someone acts lukewarm or indifferent towards you, then I hate to break it to you, sista, but they're probably not that into you. The odds are that they're not playing hard to get. And they are unlikely to change the longer you sit around waiting for them.

Tough love

The good news is that this is not your fault. You can't make people fall in love with you any more than the next girl can. Your crush is probably not a bad person, either; it's just that you're not the one your crush is looking for. And the even better news? The sooner you recognise this, the sooner you'll be free to move on and find someone who is worthy of your love and attention. Someone who will care for you completely rather than conditionally. And you deserve that, don't you? You should be appreciated and valued for the rock star you are and to find someone who will treasure you for all your great qualities. It's just not this person. Sorry.

This might seem like a lot of tough love. But saying that one person doesn't love you is not the same as saying you're unloveable or that you won't ever find love. In fact, it can actually be quite liberating to acknowledge that a crush is simply just not that into you, because it frees you up from spending so much time trying to decode all those mixed messages you've been receiving.

Obviously this is easier said than done. If it was that straightforward, girls wouldn't spend so much time inventing excuses for people who give them mixed signals. (Hey, if it makes you feel any better, I once convinced myself that the only reason a boy I liked didn't want to officially date me was because he was 'too free-spirited' to settle down. Yeah, I wasn't fooling anyone.)

Reality check

> When someone shows you who they are, believe them.
>
> **Maya Angelou**[3]

Take a step back and objectively review all the information at hand. People generally show us who they are, but it's up to us to believe them. Consider *all* of this person's words and actions (not just the nice stuff) with an honest eye. Have you been choosing to ignore anything because it doesn't fit your happily-ever-after fantasies? Have you made excuses to justify inconsistent or just-not-that-into-you behaviour? If so, you wouldn't be the first to do so. But remember, if someone is acting only half-interested in you, or if you're making excuses for them, then you're already working twice as hard as they are just to keep the *idea* of a future relationship alive. It's time to reassess the situation:

1. Talk to a friend who will give you an honest opinion. Often when we are really into someone our judgment can become clouded. Speaking to someone outside of the situation may provide you with a fresh perspective, because he or she can see things more clearly.
2. Spell out your expectations. If you are afraid to do this because you are worried you'll be

seen as too pushy or rushing things, then ask yourself whether this person is as open and willing to start a relationship as you are.
3. Stop making excuses for this person. Don't ignore the bad stuff. And don't invent signs that are not there. If someone's actions frequently contradict their words, or if you feel that you are constantly having to explain away their inconsistent behaviour to friends (or yourself), stepping back will help you to reflect and gain clarity on what is really going on.
4. Spend some time with friends and others who ground you and make you feel good about yourself. Put yourself first for a while. Remind yourself of what it's like to feel in control of your life.

Finally, if you're really struggling to work out whether or not someone is into you, the following checklist should help. If you tick three or more boxes, it might be time to reconsider the relationship:

- ❏ They don't want to call you their girlfriend.
- ❏ They say they are not the relationship type/are too busy for a relationship/do not believe in commitment.
- ❏ They forget things that are important to you, or important dates like your birthday.

- ❏ They won't hold your hand in public.
- ❏ They never initiate any calls or text exchanges themselves.
- ❏ They don't make you feel appreciated or special.
- ❏ You never feel that you know where you stand with them.
- ❏ They don't take the time to have those 'getting to know you' conversations with you or spend any quality time alone with just you.
- ❏ They want to 'keep it casual', see you more as a friend (or a 'friend with benefits') and want to be able to hook up with other people.
- ❏ They have trouble scheduling anything with you more than a day in advance.
- ❏ They talk about their ex constantly.
- ❏ They don't give you many compliments.
- ❏ You sometimes feel they use you. They seem to only want one thing from you.
- ❏ They don't confide in you or seek your advice on things that are important to them.
- ❏ They aren't there when you really need them.
- ❏ They don't make it crystal clear how they feel about you.

The just too into you

Sometimes the opposite can occur. There is a good chance that at some point in your life, you will come across someone who is way more interested in you than you are in them.

Crushing dilemmas: what happens when the feelings are not mutual?

Knowing how to turn down someone who has a big ol' crush on you can be pretty difficult, particularly if you want to remain friends or feel worried about hurting the person's feelings.

During my life, there have been a couple of times when I've met a really lovely guy who has developed feelings for me that I just didn't return. It was no-one's fault; the chemistry just wasn't right and it wasn't meant to be. When I was younger, I didn't handle this situation very well. I would often try to avoid the person. Once or twice, I even tried being mean to the guy in the hopes that it would turn him off. (That didn't work, by the way; it just made everyone else think I was a cruel and heartless cow.) Another time, I was so determined to remain friends with the guy that I ignored what was going on and played dumb about his crush. This only gave him false hope and ultimately caused even more pain for both of us. As I've got older, I've become *slightly* better at learning to let the would-be Romeos down gently yet firmly, but I'll admit that this is not the easiest part of dating. If you're struggling with how to let someone down:

- Remember that this person's heart is on the line, so put some thought into what to say. It can be really helpful to write down why you don't feel the same way, as this may help to give you some clarity.
- Use 'I' statements ('I think ...', 'I feel ...'), as that is the kindest way to speak your truth.

- Be tactful. For example, it sounds much more insulting to say to someone, 'I find you boring' than 'I find that our interests are just too different.'
- If the person tries to win you over but you are definite about your feelings, don't be swayed. Just because someone likes you, it doesn't mean you have to go out with that person. Stand firm and calmly repeat what you've said about the reasons you don't think it will work for you.
- If you think the message isn't getting through, write to them. Again, be sure to use 'I' statements and write in a compassionate way. Imagining how you might feel in the other person's shoes will help.[4]

The guys who have had one-way crushes on me have mostly been respectful of my feelings. They expressed their disappointment with gentle honesty, wished me well in life, and in time they moved on and found girls who made them far happier than I ever could have. These guys were all princes and I still think of them as great guys to this day.

Not everyone handles rejection so gracefully, though. Rejection does hurt and it is fairly normal for someone to feel a bit disappointed or sad if you don't want to pursue a relationship with them. But this is no excuse for bad behaviour on their part. Not ever. Nor is it OK for people to continue to make unwanted advances towards you if you have let them know you're not into them. It's not just bad manners, it can actually be a form of harassment or stalking.

Sometimes girls laugh when stalking is mentioned because of all the associated connotations. I get that. But on a serious note, it can be very distressing if someone is harassing you or won't leave you alone. If this happens and you find you are feeling tense, anxious or upset, then you need to speak to an adult you trust and then cut off contact with the person.

If someone who likes you keeps contacting or checking up on you when you don't want them to, and it causes you discomfort or distress, that's stalking. They might constantly text, call or harass you through social media. They might turn up or hang out at places where they expect you to be or try to contact your friends to find out information about you. In some cases, they might interfere with your property or spread malicious gossip about you. Stalking is a serious crime and can be reported to the police.

Most people who use stalking tactics are male and most already know the person they target through school, work, previous relationships or friendship networks. Of course, you wouldn't know this from the movies. Just look at how many stalker films reinforce the stereotypical image of the creepy *stranger* stalker who lurks in the shadows and spies on women through binoculars. Or what about the social misfit who lives in his mother's basement and smells like cheese?

The problem with these exaggerated stereotypes is that they divert our attention away from the far more common type of stalker: familiar, normal-looking guys who are already known to girls, such as ex-boyfriends, former friends or work colleagues.

What's worse, Hollywood treats stalking by these kinds of men as either a joke or romantic.

> In romcoms, it's considered terribly romantic for a guy to show up at your office and deliver a passionate monologue about how much he loves you, in front of all your co-workers and your boss. Even after you've told him that it's over and you never want to see him again. If a guy did that in real life, you'd be horrified ... But in romcoms, that kind of thing is totally standard.
> **Chloe Angyal**[5]

One day Danni and I went to the movies and watched a major blockbuster that had just been released. It included a scene where the lead male character told the lead female character that he followed her home every day and watched her from afar. A group of teen girls was sitting in front of us and one of them yelled out, 'Eww! Stalker, much?' Even though the scene was meant to be seen as romantic, they all saw straight through it and recognised the creep factor immediately. Solid work, ladies!

Like the girls in the movie theatre, you can also call

out creepy behaviour or actions that cross the line. For me, my policy is that if a person's actions are making someone feel uneasy or uncomfortable, then those actions are crossing a line. It's a great test to apply to any situation because it's so simple. Combined with the other tools you've learnt in this chapter, you're now better equipped to spot a range of dating pitfalls when you come across them!

Quiz

Circle the answer that comes closest to describing your situation.

1. You've been crushing on someone at the school bus stop for months now, but they don't seem to know you exist. You:

- A. Keep pining away. Maybe one day they'll notice you.
- B. Take photos of your crush when they are not looking. Your crush is just so darn cute!
- C. Talk to your crush. That way you can suss out whether they are interested, and if not, you can move on.

2. You've been dating someone for three weeks, but every time you suggest spending time with your family or friends they change the subject or make up an excuse. You also haven't been introduced to any

of their friends or family. It's really beginning to bug you. You:

- A. Ignore the issue. Hopefully they will change.
- B. Organise to meet up at the movies and ... Surprise! All your friends turn up, too!
- C. Talk to them about it. Your family and friends are important to you and you should be able to raise the issue.

3. A friend complains to you that her ex won't stop texting her. You:

- A. Wish your ex would make that sort of gesture.
- B. Think she is overreacting. She can be such a drama queen.
- C. Listen to her and take her seriously. She needs your support.

4. The difference between a stalker and a secret admirer is:

- A. How cute they are!
- B. Whether they smell like cheese.
- C. Whether you feel comfortable. A harmless crush causes no discomfort or distress.

5. The person you're dating is sending mixed messages. They blow hot and cold and you can never work out where you stand. You:

- A. Give it time and convince yourself that it will all work out in the end.

Crushing dilemmas: what happens when the feelings are not mutual?

    B.   Start turning up at places you expect them to be in order to spend more time together. It's the only way to move things forward.

    C.   Honestly review all of their behaviour before talking to a friend who will give you a balanced opinion.

6. If someone asks you out in a respectful way, but you're just not that interested, you should:

    A.   Awkwardly change the subject and hope they get the message.

    B.   Lie. Tell them you've already got plans.

    C.   Remember that their heart is on the line and the kindest thing is to give a tactful but truthful response.

7. To me, a good relationship would feel:

    A.   Like a romance novel. Full of fantasy.

    B.   Like a romcom. Full of drama!

    C.   Like coming home. Caring, loving and safe.

Now add up how many A's, B's and C's you circled, and check below.

Mostly A's

You fancy yourself quite the romantic and you genuinely believe that things will eventually work out for the best in the end. But sometimes your romantic sensibilities cloud your judgment and you avoid important conversations that need to be had. Remember, learning to assert yourself is an important skill in any relationship.

Mostly B's

Your life is probably full of drama, which on some level you enjoy. But be careful. Whether you intend to or not, you may be crossing other people's boundaries and making them feel as though you don't really respect their wishes. In the long run, you risk pushing them away from you.

Mostly C's

Hello, Oh-wise-one. You have a lot of this relationship stuff down pat, don't you? You know how to support your friends and you give good advice. You're honest with yourself and others and you're willing to assert yourself and have some of the tough conversations. Good work, you!

Affirmations

I attract only healthy, loving people into my life.

I contribute to the healthy growth of my relationships.

I deserve fulfilling, nurturing relationships.

CHAPTER 4

Deal makers and deal breakers
by Nina

Have you ever noticed how many love stories imply that love needs to be dramatic or even dangerous in order for it to be exciting? Consider all the violence and drama in *Romeo and Juliet*, for example. And have you noticed how love stories, particularly the vampire-themed ones, tend to connect passion and sex to violence and danger? In fact, the more blood and violence there is surrounding a relationship, the more sexy and exciting their love is supposed to be. This is what is called 'romanticising' violence: it's the idea that there is something erotic and titillating about danger and even brutality.

Flirting with danger
Pop stars are also constantly singing about loving 'bad boys' and men who are 'dangerous' or 'toxic'.

Even perfume bottles celebrate the darker aspects of relationships. Think about some of the popular perfume names: Envy, Obsession, Fierce. There are also perfumes named Full Choke, Dangerous, Unforgivable Woman and Hypnotic Poison — how romantic! Can you imagine a perfume bottle called Consideration: by Calvin Klein or Compromise: by Tommy Hilfiger? Probably not. Apparently these relationship qualities aren't nearly as interesting or sexy!

The truth is that our culture has some pretty strange ideas about what passes for romance. Take dear old *Beauty and the Beast*. On the surface, the story is all about inner beauty and seeing through exterior appearances (provided it's the dude who is ugly, that is). But even the sugary-sweet Disney version of the tale has some dark undertones: the Beast locks Belle in his castle, isolates her from her family, violently smashes up the place and verbally abuses her. Domestic violence, anyone? Belle's only other love alternative is Gaston, a rude, arrogant and cruel man who tries to blackmail her into marriage. Apparently the best choices on offer for Belle are an abuser and a jerk.

While I love me a good fairy tale, the thing I find most disturbing about this particular story is the subtext that women who stick it out with violent men will ultimately be rewarded. It's also rubbish to suggest that with a bit of patience and tender loving care, aggressive and abusive men will change their violent ways. (So you know, most abusive men get more violent, not less violent over time.)

Now let's turn our attention to *Sleeping Beauty* and *Snow White and the Seven Dwarfs*. Since when is kissing unconscious women considered acceptable, let alone romantic? (Hello! Consent issues!) In fact, in the original version of *Sleeping Beauty*, the handsome prince (who was actually a married and adulterous king) did a lot more than just kiss the unconscious maiden. He sexually assaulted her and nine months later, while still unconscious, she gave birth to twins. Talk about a fairy-tale fail!

So as you have probably gathered by now, our culture doesn't always promote the most healthy examples of romantic relationships. But there is good news here. For starters, you're probably already skilled at deconstructing the ads, TV shows, movies and books around you, right? Next time you see a romcom on TV or at the movies, afterwards try deconstructing the way it portrayed romance and gender roles. It's even more fun if you do it with friends.

The second bit of good news is that our values aren't only shaped by what we watch and read. When it comes to intimate relationships, our values are shaped by a number of forces, the most powerful of which is the relationships we see around us while growing up, particularly those within our families. Obviously not every family is perfect and not all relationships which have been modelled for us are going to be ideal. So let's talk about what makes a good relationship. Here are some signs:

- **Trust.** You trust each other to stick to what you say and you both feel you can rely on each other.
- **Respect.** Not only do you respect each other's boundaries, you also respect and admire each other as people.
- **Giving space.** You can each give the other space to do your own thing and are not overly clingy or dependent. You are both happy in yourselves.
- **Positive support.** You support each other in life and help each other work towards your goals.
- **Quiet times together.** You're both happy to chill out in each other's company and feel that you can be yourself around each other.
- **Having fun.** You can laugh and have a lot of fun together. You enjoy spending time in each other's company and doing things, including socialising, together.
- **Good communication skills.** You each really listen to what the other is talking about and are interested in what the other has to say about things. You enjoy hearing each other's opinions and feel comfortable

voicing your views, even if you disagree sometimes.
- **Good conflict-resolution skills.** No couple is without conflict, unless one person has become a doormat (which is never a good sign). The trick is knowing how to resolve conflict in a fair and peaceful manner — for more on this, see Chapter 9.
- **Fair financials.** Neither one of you takes advantage of the other financially, tries to control the other person's finances or expects to have your way paid for you.
- **Physical comfort.** You feel physically comfortable around each other, and you can openly communicate about the intimate side of your relationship.
- **Room to grow.** Happy couples accept that people change, as do their personalities. You each allow the other the space to grow as a person and explore new activities.

That list is a good starting point, but often it can be helpful to hear what other girls have to say based on their own experiences, true? I also love hearing from girls who are in that loved-up lovey-dovey stage because they are just bursting with joy! So here is what a few teen girls said about what a good relationship looks like to them:

My boyfriend sends a text to me every morning saying, 'Good Morning Beautiful.' He always listens and understands and makes me laugh every day.

Catie, 15

He doesn't just say 'I love you' — he means it and shows it. He doesn't just think I am beautiful, he also thinks I am strong, smart and funny, too! We share the same beliefs and outlook on life, too. It's all about the mutual respect and ability to have fun and support each other through the ups and downs.

Kate, 19

He is wonderful if he holds your hand in public, puts you before his friends, won't let anyone's opinions of you affect his perception of you.

Selena, 15

He is the one who holds my hand when I'm scared and comes to me for comfort, too. He's a feminist and stands beside me and helps me fight for everything that's important to me.

Tess, 19

He loves me for who I am, without make-up, in any clothes, before I brush my hair in the morning. Just as I am.

Paris, 15

When a relationship turns toxic

Sometimes a relationship might feel good at the beginning but then begin to change.

When we first started dating, it was incredibly romantic, and after only three dates Ben told me he loved me. It was intense from the beginning. We would speak every day and see each other every spare moment we had. He was full of compliments and paid a lot of attention to me, and it felt wonderful. But Ben also had a dark side. He would get extremely jealous of any other guys and he'd also put my friends down and make fun of them behind their backs.

About a year into our relationship things suddenly began to get worse. When we went out with his friends, Ben would tell me what to wear. Around this time we started fighting more and more, and I heard a rumour he was cheating on me. I was unhappy but I felt trapped and unable to leave because he always knew exactly what to say to make me stay. I felt so guilty for even thinking about leaving.

Eventually we broke up. He kept texting me and calling me. He was good friends with my brother so he kept popping up at our house to hang out with him. I tried to tell him I needed space but he didn't listen. I started dating someone new and when he found out, he sent me another text calling me a *'slut' and he started spreading rumours about me to our mutual friends. In the end, my dad had to go round there and speak to him, and I had to block him on Facebook.*

Shelly, 19 (names have been changed)

Looking back, Shelly says that the warning signs were there from the beginning. He got too invested in the relationship too quickly. When it came to hanging out with the opposite sex, he had one set of rules for himself and another set for her. He embedded himself in her family but isolated her from her friends and anyone who didn't approve of him. He was controlling of her and ignored her feelings on numerous occasions.

Girls and women who experience a relationship like this sometimes blame themselves for not ending it soon enough. But did you notice how incredibly charming Ben was at the beginning of the relationship? And did you notice how he made Shelly feel guilty and ashamed about even thinking of leaving? The reality is that someone like Ben works hard at cutting his partner off from her friends and undermining her confidence as a way of gaining power over her. It's really important that we support people who are in controlling or harmful relationships by realising that it's not their fault. If you are worried about your own relationship or the relationship of a friend, read over the following checklist. If you tick any of the boxes or if the list brings up any issues for you, speak to an adult you trust as soon as you can. There is also a list of resources at the back of this book.

Does your partner:
- act jealous or possessive?
- falsely accuse you of cheating?
- ever try to isolate you from your friends or family?
- put you down or tell you no-one else would want you?
- threaten to self-harm if you leave?
- go through your phone, email or personal belongings?
- seek to control whom you connect with on social media or insist you 'unfriend' certain people?
- criticise the way you look or tell you how to dress or do your hair?
- try to control your actions? (For example, by telling you what to eat or where to go.)
- compare you negatively to other girls or people they have dated?
- ever act more like a parent than a partner?
- ever pressure you to do things sexually?
- ever make degrading or sexist comments about women in general?
- ever blame you for him losing his temper? (For example, 'You shouldn't provoke me like that!')
- humiliate you?

- ❑ want to know where you are at all times or get mad if you can't be reached on the phone?
- ❑ try to control how you spend money or want to know all the details about your finances?
- ❑ ever give you the silent treatment?
- ❑ ever have unpredictable mood swings?
- ❑ say things that make you feel good, but do things that make you feel bad?
- ❑ twist your words against you?
- ❑ say something and then deny or contradict it, making you feel as though you are going crazy?
- ❑ ever get physically aggressive? (For example, by throwing things, hitting walls, driving recklessly to frighten you, or hurting or threatening you, other people or pets.)

Do you:

- ❑ ever feel afraid to bring up certain topics in front of your partner?
- ❑ ever feel like you're walking on eggshells?
- ❑ often feel manipulated by your partner?
- ❑ ever feel scared or intimidated by your partner?
- ❑ constantly make excuses to other people for the way your partner acts, or conceal aspects of your partner's behaviour?
- ❑ believe you can help your partner change if only you changed something about yourself?
- ❑ try to avoid doing anything that might set your partner off?

- ever feel that no matter what you do, your partner will never be totally happy with you?
- do what your partner wants you to do instead of what you want?
- stay with your partner because you are afraid of what would happen if you broke up?

How to get the love you deserve: the traffic-light system

> Good relationships feel good. They feel right. They don't hurt. They're not painful. That's not just with somebody you want to marry, but it's with the friends that you choose. It's with the people you surround yourselves with.
> **Michelle Obama**[1]

When I was younger, I carried around a checklist of what I was looking for in an ideal partner. It specified everything, right down to his height, eye and hair colour, dress style and musical taste. (Obviously he also had to be popular, funny and smart — that was a given.) This checklist of mine wasn't actually written down on a physical piece of paper. It didn't need to be. I'd gone over it so many times in my mind, it was well and truly seared into my memory.

Looking back, I don't think I was that unusual. A lot of girls carry around a mental list of ideal criteria they are looking for in a partner. But my list had two problems. First, in some areas, such as looks, it was waaaay too picky. Physical attraction is really important in a relationship, and it's not at all shallow to be attracted to certain physical characteristics — it's just that you don't need to define every single aspect of your ideal partner's appearance right down to the brand of shoes they wear. My second problem was that while I'd gone into a lot of detail in some areas, such as the CDs he should own, I'd forgotten to add some of the really important stuff that should be in any relationship, such as trust, companionship and respect. It's not that I didn't want or value those things; I definitely wanted them. It's just that I had a very general sort of idea about that stuff rather than a concrete list of characteristics that make up a good relationship.

I guess I just assumed that when I met my ideal (looking) guy, he would come magically equipped with all those skills and qualities that make for a good partner, such as being loving and caring and a good listener. It doesn't always work out that way, and a person can be great on paper while being a disaster in a relationship.

So if you've got one of those lists yourself, put it aside for one moment and concentrate on this question: what do you think a good relationship should *feel* like? How would you know if you were in one?

Now take an A4 piece of paper and turn it sideways. Divide it into three columns. Label the three columns 'Red', 'Yellow' and 'Green', and follow the steps below.

Relationship red light: the deal breakers

A deal breaker is something that you aren't willing to compromise your standards on in a relationship, no matter what. What are your relationship deal breakers? Your no-exceptions, no-excuses rules? Lack of trust, honesty and respect should be on the list — but beyond those, not everyone's deal breakers will be the same. Sometimes people may even have polar opposite deal breakers — for instance, one person expects to have children one day and the other person doesn't.

The important thing is to work out what your own deal breakers are, then write them down in the Red column.

> From a relationship I absolutely expect honesty and trust. They are the main things that two people should have in a relationship or it won't work out.
>
> Amber, 16

> I need to be able to speak freely in a relationship, without being judged or feeling awkward.
>
> Paris, 15

> I think the most important thing in a relationship is loyalty, trust and respect. Each go hand in hand, really. Without these three, a healthy relationship would be nonexistent.
>
> Alice, 19

I expect to always feel safe, never feel scared, and have a lot of fun along the way.

Lisa, 18

A deal breaker for me is [if] the person [isn't] genuine. I don't want someone who changes depending on who they are around. They need to be happy and proud of who they are.

Jess, 16

A deal breaker for me would be a guy who didn't respect women (not just me but other women). If he was a chauvinist, if he made lots of sexist jokes, or if he put womanhood down, then that would be my deal breaker.

Nisha, 18

My deal breaker would be if they were self-destructive or if they had an addiction or a gambling problem.

Sophie, 19

My deal breaker would be if my boyfriend cheated on me.

Tania, 14

The deal breaker for me is not showing respect and having patience, as well as understanding my choices.

Fleur, 16

They should never pressure you or ask you to do something you're not comfortable with. That would be my deal breaker.

Emma, 17

A deal breaker for me is someone who is manipulative. It's so detrimental to your emotional wellbeing. Someone who is manipulative does not have your happiness at heart but wishes to control you through guilt and shame. Total deal breaker!

Alice, 19

Infidelity, abuse of any kind, lying and a relationship where I can't be me [are deal breakers].

Erika, 16

Relationship yellow light: negotiables

Now fill your Yellow column. Yellow lights are things that you are willing to compromise on or make an allowance for in a relationship. It's important to work out your *own* line between your deal breakers and negotiables, as these will be different for everyone. Ask yourself: how important is this issue to me?

To get you started, weigh up whether it is a deal breaker or negotiable that your partner:

- gets along with your family
- likes your friends

- shares the same spiritual or religious beliefs as you (including if you're an atheist)
- shares the same political beliefs as you
- values education
- is good with money
- likes the same hobbies and activities that you do
- has a fit and active lifestyle
- shares your outlook on divisive issues (for example, abortion, vegetarianism, pornography)
- makes similar choices as you do when it comes to alcohol and other drugs
- is very physically attractive
- is able to see you as frequently as you would like
- shares the same view as you on commitment and relationship styles
- enjoys the same sorts of movies as you
- laughs at the same things you do

Relationship green light: ideals

These are the things you seek out in an ideal relationship. They aren't essential to a relationship, but you would like your ideal partner to have these qualities, such as being really into the same sport as you or having a passion for the same hobby that you love.

When you have finished writing down all of the ideals you can think of, reflect on what you have written.

What values really jump out as important to you? You might want to ask your parents about what their deal breakers, negotiables and ideals are in a relationship. Talking it over with people who love you and also have years of relationship experience under their belts can help you refine your ideas even further.

Once you've finished, put your traffic-light system somewhere safe. It can be a useful guide for you to look back on whenever you start dating someone new to see how they fit in with your values. Once you know what you really want, you'll be much more confident spotting the right relationship for you.

Quiz

Tick the boxes that best describe your situation.

Is my relationship healthy?	Or is my relationship unhealthy?
Does my partner make me feel good? ❑ My partner listens to me and values my opinions. ❑ My partner believes in me and supports my goals. ❑ My partner does kind things for me.	*Does my partner put me down?* ❑ My partner tells me I am stupid or crazy. ❑ My partner blames me for everything that goes wrong. ❑ My partner calls me names. ❑ My partner dismisses what I say.

Is my relationship healthy?	Or is my relationship unhealthy?
Does my partner make me feel safe? ❏ My partner can talk about their frustrations without trying to intimidate me. ❏ My partner asks me how I am feeling. ❏ My partner says it's OK if we disagree sometimes.	*Does my partner lie?* ❏ My partner cheats on me. ❏ My partner lies about their actions. ❏ My partner lies about hurting me.
Does my partner respect me? ❏ My partner likes me the way I am. ❏ My partner asks me what I think about things. ❏ My partner wants me to succeed. ❏ My partner is happy for me to try new things.	*Does my partner try to scare me?* ❏ My partner threatens to hurt me or him/herself. ❏ My partner makes me do things I don't want to do. ❏ My partner yells at me.
Does my partner trust and support me? ❏ My partner thinks it's OK when I spend time with my friends. ❏ My partner supports me trying new things. ❏ My partner believes me when I say I am faithful.	*Does my partner try to control me?* ❏ My partner won't let me see my friends or tries to keep me away from them. ❏ My partner wants to know where I am all the time. ❏ My partner gets easily jealous.

Is my relationship healthy?	Or is my relationship unhealthy?
Is my partner honest? ❏ My partner admits mistakes. ❏ My partner sticks to our agreements. ❏ My partner tells the truth.	*Does my partner try to hurt me?* ❏ My partner pushes, shoves, grabs, hits or kicks me. ❏ My partner makes me do sexual things when I don't want to. ❏ My partner makes me do illegal things.

*Adapted from www.leapsf.org with permission.[2]

Affirmations

I allow love to flow to me and through me. I allow myself to be loved fully.

I am worthy of love.

I deserve to be treated with compassion, dignity and respect.

CHAPTER 5

So you're dating! Now what?

by Nina

When you meet someone you like and the feelings are mutual, life feels exhilarating. Your spirit soars and dances. It's no wonder so many songs and poems are written about love. So once you're sailing, how do you keep your own little love boat afloat? In this chapter we're going to look at a thing called boundaries: what they are, and how they can help prevent your relationship from unexpectedly capsizing. We'll also look at why some people get swamped in relationships (I bet you know of at least one girl this has happened to) and what you can do to avoid this situation yourself. And the great thing is that the principles you'll learn in this chapter can be applied to other types of relationships, including your friendships and relationships with brothers or sisters and so on.

What are boundaries?

Have you ever had someone take something of yours without asking? Has someone ever gone through your diary or private text messages without your permission? Or what about this: have you ever had someone walk in on you while you were on the toilet? Eeep!

Welcome to the world of boundaries. In your day-to-day life you're probably already familiar with friends and family members who sometimes cross your boundaries. Like your sister who keeps taking your favourite skirt without asking, or the shop assistant who has no problem opening the change-room door while you're standing in your underwear. (Is it just me, or does this always happen at the worst possible moment?)

When people ask very intrusive questions or share Too Much Information, they are crossing our privacy boundaries. People can also cross our physical boundaries by acting overly familiar with us when we have only just met them — they might behave in a very touchy way or do something that feels too forward, like eating food off your plate without asking (STOP! Put down the donut, back away slowly and no-one needs to get hurt!). Friends can cross our boundaries, too, such as when one friend starts copying everything you say and do, from your hair style to your unique taste in music. I once had a girl tell me that her best friend was copying every little thing about her, even the way she sneezed!

When it comes to romantic relationships, knowing how to maintain and respect boundaries gets more complicated. Drinking out of someone's glass or touching them affectionately can be a way for people to flirt and show that they are comfortable with each other. But people sometimes do these things to speed up intimacy with someone they have only just met, without really paying attention to what the other person wants or if they feel comfortable.

In relationships, learning to set and maintain boundaries around your body, privacy, belongings, emotions and time is not about keeping other people out. It's actually the exact opposite. It's about establishing clear guidelines so that you can let people in without being smothered by them.

> My daughter had a new boyfriend who she was obviously smitten with. She was calling him and Facebook chatting him virtually all night ... often up until 3 a.m.! I kept cautioning her that it was too much, too soon, especially as she would often say things like 'He's not replying, I better send another message in case my last one didn't get through.' After about a week his mother rang and spoke to me, warning that unless Simone stopped contacting him so often, she was going to have to ban them from seeing each other as apparently her son was getting in lots of trouble for not doing homework and was starting to tell his family he felt smothered.
>
> I explained to my daughter that when someone is not replying as frequently as we'd like them

> to, or offering extended responses, it may mean they want to limit the communication. It doesn't necessarily mean they don't like you a lot, too, but that they just need more space. Although she was very hurt at first and took this as rejection, she agreed to suggest that they limit themselves to only talking/texting/messaging between 9 and 10 every night. It then became a time they both looked forward to, and she found he started telling her how much he missed her at times, too. Plus, I think it gave him more time to think about what he'd like to say, as talking didn't come as naturally to him as it did to her!

Annabel, mother of Simone, 17

It's normal that when two people start going out they want to spend a lot of time together (the same goes with BFFs). Of course when you meet someone great you want to soak up their goodness! But it's also important to maintain a sense of identity outside of the relationship. Here are some signs you might be struggling with how to maintain your individual sense of self:

- copying the other person's taste in things such as music or copying the way the person speaks, acts or dresses
- getting anxious when your partner doesn't immediately text or call you back

- spending little time with your other friends or spending time only with your partner and their friends
- losing sight of personal goals or cutting back on activities that make you happy, so that you can spend all your time and energy on your partner
- lying to your friends and family about aspects of the new relationship
- doing things that go against your principles while with your partner, such as taking drugs, getting drunk or getting into a car with someone who has been drinking

New relationships, new boundaries

In new relationships, setting boundaries around how much time you spend with your partner will actually help keep the spark between you fresh.

> Boundaries for me weren't just physical. I was in my final year of high school and was really committed to my studies — some would say it was my first love.
>
> I only had a few months of hard study to go and I knew anyone that really liked me for me would respect my school lovin' ways! Plus, I didn't want seeing this boy to become just another thing on my daily 'to do' list ...
>
> When I put it to him that way, he was very understanding. I would let him know what I had on

for the week and we would work out times to see each other. Our plans weren't set in stone, though. If something came up between 9 and 3.30 that desperately needed my attention I would just let him know. Some weeks I might see him twice and then nothing for another ten days, but at least that way seeing him was something I could look forward to. Once the school days were over and results were released I was happy with my decision to prioritise ... plus the four months of holidays before I headed off to uni were the best I ever had because I could let go of my first love with no regrets.

Jemma, 19

How cool is that? A girl who has clear goals for herself and has worked out how to balance life, personal ambitions and a relationship. Below are some other boundaries to be aware of. As you are reading through them, see if you can think of a time when someone you know has pushed one of your boundaries. How did it make you feel and what steps did you take to manage the situation?

Property. Do you have a friend who borrows pens from your pencil case without returning them? Or has someone ever damaged or hid your property in order to hurt you? Someone is crossing your property boundaries when they borrow, use or take something of yours without asking you, or interfere with your property in order to upset you. Exes sometimes interfere with property as a way of expressing their anger. Remember, it's not OK for people to mess with your goods!

Money. Does the person you're dating constantly borrow money from you? Do you always expect your date to pay your way? Remember, it's not the 1950s! If either scenario is true for your relationship, then someone's money boundaries are being crossed and it won't be long before resentment builds up. Money boundaries can also be crossed when someone makes a point of paying for everything as a way of trying to make the other person feel indebted to them.

Time. Feeling smothered? Feeling as though you never have a moment alone? When someone dominates your schedule or wants to see you so often that it prevents you from engaging in activities that you ordinarily enjoy, they are crossing your time boundaries. In more extreme cases they might make plans involving you without asking — and then get angry or lay a guilt trip on you when you try to say no. They might turn up uninvited at your home, or where you work or like to hang, expecting you to spend time with them. They might constantly text or call in order to demand your time and attention. This is a serious issue in dating and is often a sign of controlling behaviour. These boundaries can also be breached if someone constantly disrespects the value of your time by always being late or breaking plans at the last minute. If this is sounding familiar, it's time to reset the boundaries, stat!

Privacy. If someone snoops through your bag, diary, mobile phone or social media accounts without your permission, they're crossing your <u>privacy boundaries</u> (and behaving like a mega stalker, too). Other ways someone can cross these boundaries are by insisting that you show them whom you are texting or chatting to, and then getting angry if you don't. They might demand that you tell them private information, such as where you've been and whom you've been with. This is possessive, controlling behaviour and a huge red flag for the relationship. You should speak to a parent or other adult you trust about this as soon as possible.

Emotions. We all know people who use emotionally manipulative strategies to get what they want. They might need constant emotional reassurance from you or always expect you to 'manage' their emotional dramas. This can be very taxing. Your <u>emotional boundaries</u> can also be crossed if someone ignores your emotions altogether, belittles your feelings or disregards your opinions. Someone disrespects their partner's emotional boundaries when they repeatedly lie, get jealous, or use guilt, emotional blackmail, verbal putdowns or other forms of manipulation. This might include sulking or getting upset when they don't get their way, making threats like 'I couldn't live if you broke up with me', or being mean and insensitive.

Physical. If someone invades your personal space or physically intimidates you, they're crossing your physical boundaries. This can also occur if someone interferes with your physical wellbeing — for instance, by pressuring you to use alcohol or other drugs, or by tricking you into consuming these substances, for example by drink spiking. Other types of behaviour that crosses your physical boundaries are when someone threatens, endangers or actually harms you, such as speeding in a car, physically intimidating you, or pushing, shoving, grabbing or slapping you. As part of your physical boundaries, you also have sexual boundaries. This is a really important topic that will be explored in a lot more detail in the next chapter.

Relationship reset

Sometimes people cross our boundaries by accident (like walking in on you while you're on the toilet!). But boundaries can also get crossed when someone engages in manipulative behaviour. If you find that you have difficulty saying no to someone, or if you feel someone is constantly crossing the line or trying to control or manipulate you in some way, there are things you can do to reassert your boundaries.

Boundaries are different for each individual and couple, so firstly spend some time reflecting and deciding what is acceptable to you. Write down your boundaries and review them, so you can communicate these clearly to your partner. A good indication that your boundaries might be being crossed is if you feel stressed or resentful after spending time with your partner, if you have a 'gut feel' that something isn't right for you, or if you feel exhausted and worried about talking to or seeing your partner. For example, you may only want to spend one evening during the school week with the person you're dating, but they want to see you every night. It is up to you to stand your ground. Take responsibility to be firm.

- Find a calm and quiet moment to talk to your partner about boundaries. Don't spring the conversation on your partner when you are angry or in a fight. Say something like 'I want to discuss some needs I've got, to make this relationship even better.'
- Use 'I' statements and avoid saying 'you' when you define the problem. For example, instead of saying, 'You are crowding me', which is likely to get your partner on the defensive, you might say, 'I feel crowded when I don't have any time to myself.'
- Reassure your partner that you like or love them (if you do!) but say that some of the

ways you act with each other need to change so you'll feel even happier.
- Be prepared with specific, recent examples that help you illustrate the issue. Explain how those situations made you feel (using 'I' statements).
- You might have been thinking about this for ages, but it might come as a shock to your partner, so give them some time to process things. Allow them to make suggestions, too, so that you can negotiate.
- If you find it difficult to articulate your issues, write a list and then share them with your partner that way.
- Notice when your partner breaches the new 'rules' and remind them gently. Also acknowledge and thank your partner when they respect your boundaries.
- If your partner continually does something you've asked them not to do, it might be time to question your relationship.[1]

Respecting your partner's boundaries

Your partner's boundaries can be crossed in much the same ways that your own boundaries can.

It drives me crazy when my girlfriend flirts with my best mate. I trust them both, I do, and they

> say it's just for fun but it still upsets me. A lot.
> And I am not even allowed to show this or they
> tease me for being jealous.

Michael, 15

> My girlfriend gets really jealous really easily.
> She sulks when I say I want to spend time with
> other people and if I don't text her as soon as
> she texts me she freaks out and then will accuse
> me of not caring enough about her. It really
> stresses me out and makes me feel completely
> smothered. I still really care about her, but it's
> really bad.

Edward, 17

Just as we expect and are entitled to be treated with respect, we also have an obligation to treat others with respect. It can be hard for others to tell us that they are unhappy with the way they are being treated. In that case, listen carefully and pay attention to their actions. People will tell us in all sorts of ways when they are unhappy.

It takes a strong person to admit when they need to change something about how they are relating to others. If you think you might be overstepping your partner's boundaries or being manipulative, step back and reflect on how things have been going. Ask yourself whether you would be happy being treated that way and, more importantly, whether *your partner* is happy.

Speak to them about it and listen with an open heart to what they have to say, even if it stings a bit. You might also want to speak to a trusted adult who will give you honest feedback.

Just as you learn to be a good friend through practice, good relationships also take practice. No-one knows all there is to know about being the perfect partner straight off and it's OK to make mistakes if we are open to learning from them. And remember, the real key to having a successful relationship is knowing yourself, respecting and caring for your partner, and having an expectation of being treated with care and respect.

Quiz

Circle the answer that comes closest to describing your situation.

1. Your partner wants you to see a movie together but you've already promised your best friend that you will see the same movie with her and that it will be just the two of you. You:

- A. Say yes to your partner and tell your friend that you're really sorry but something came up.
- B. See the movie twice and wear the cost.
- C. Tell your partner that you've already got plans to see the movie with someone else. Then offer to see a different movie instead.

2. You're on a first date with someone you've been crushing on for ages. They are driving and start speeding recklessly. It's beginning to scare you. You:

    A. Hold on extra tight! You're almost home, anyway, and you don't want to appear uptight about it. Besides, they're probably just trying to impress you.

    B. Tell them you've got motion sickness. And if that doesn't work, say there's a speed camera coming up ahead.

    C. Own it. Tell them that they're speeding and it's not cool.

3. Your boyfriend said he'd call you when he got home from a camping weekend away. You can see from Facebook that he must already be home because he's posting on other people's walls. You call him and he doesn't pick up his phone. You:

    A. Panic. Text him and ask him to call you ASAP. You want to know why he hasn't contacted you yet!

    B. Casually comment on his Facebook wall ... about twenty times! His phone might be dead, and this way he's sure to reply.

    C. Go and watch the telly. He'll call when he's ready.

4. You and your partner are both saving money for tickets to see your favourite band and have promised to save every cent you can. But now you've got your eye on a new pair of shoes you really want. You:

    A.   Stick to your commitment. The shoes can wait.

    B.   Buy the shoes and stash the evidence. They'll never know!

    C.   Explain why you want to buy the shoes. It's still your money, after all.

5. Your crush wants you to skip school to hang out. You:

    A.   Skip school and get notes off friends. You might not get a second chance.

    B.   Make up an excuse about why you can't, such as that you've got a doctor's appointment.

    C.   Tell your crush honestly that you don't want to skip school. Then arrange another time to hang.

6. Your boyfriend has been spending a lot more time with a female friend. You tell him it's beginning to make you feel uncomfortable. He agrees not to spend as much time with her, but then they start writing really flirty things on each other's Facebook walls. You:

    A.   Call your best friend in tears. At least you still have her.

    B.   Send the other girl a Facebook message telling her exactly what you think of chicks who try to steal other people's boyfriends.

C. Confront him about it. He's broken a serious agreement and needs to explain himself so that you can decide whether to stay or go.

Now add up how many A's, B's and C's you circled, and check below.

Mostly A's

You love the idea of romance and relationships, don't you? It's fine to be eager to make things work and to be willing to make necessary sacrifices, but be careful. If you're too eager to please, you may end up ignoring your own needs and feelings, or even come off as a bit smothering. If you find that you are never able to say no to things, you might want to review the information on setting boundaries.

Mostly B's

You seem to like it when things are travelling along smoothly and hate to rock the boat. But be careful that in your desire to avoid conflict you don't fall into the trap of dodging difficult conversations or being dishonest or manipulative to get your way. In the long run, doing that can cause heartache. Practise speaking up for yourself and using honest 'I' statements.

Mostly C's

Hello, Miss Boundaries! You're very confident at articulating what you want and what you think is fair.

Go, you! It's great that you are able to communicate effectively and that you stand up for yourself. Just remember that relationships are a two-way street, so it's wise to be able to distinguish between things that are really important to you while remaining willing to compromise on some of the less important things.

Affirmations

I set clear boundaries and expect others to stick by them.

I am allowed to say no.

I understand the boundaries I set and respect the boundaries of those around me.

CHAPTER 6

Your body, your rules: sex, power and consent

by Nina

Content warning: Before you read any further, we want to give you a heads-up that this chapter contains descriptions of sexual assault and violence that may trigger a strong emotional response in some readers, such as girls who have experienced similar things in the past. You can find places to get help listed at the back of this book.

In school, my friends and I talked a lot about sex. What would it feel like? Would it hurt? When would it happen for us? Who would be our first? We wondered about how sex would change things. How we would feel afterwards. How a guy would behave the next day, and how 'doing the deed' would impact on our social status, relationships and friendships. We all knew that we wanted to have sex some day. We knew we wanted others to like us. And we knew that whenever it finally happened, we wanted to be considered good at it.

But there were certain things we didn't know, such as how to feel confident enough to ask for what we wanted with a guy, or what we would do if we ever found ourselves in a situation where someone wanted us to do something we weren't sure about. I guess we all just assumed that it would be like in the movies: we'd meet the perfect person, fall in love and somehow we'd magically be mentally, emotionally and physically on the same page as each other. Oh, if only things were that simple!

Kissing frogs and sneaky snogs

The first time I ever kissed a guy — or, rather, the first time a guy kissed me — I wasn't prepared for it. I was in Year 8 at a party, casually chatting away to a guy I had just met, and out of nowhere his lips were suddenly hoovering mine right off. I was so shocked that I literally jumped up out of my seat. I wasn't upset exactly, just stunned to learn that the script I had in my head of how a kiss is supposed to go was obviously very different to the script he had in his head. In all the romantic comedies I'd seen, The Kiss happened at the end of a long, drawn-out courtship process. There was crescendoing music, mood lighting and, more often than not, a nice little speech to accompany the moment.

The Kiss was supposed to be perfect. It was most definitely not supposed to happen with some random boy, five minutes into a conversation, with my friends sitting around watching (awkward!). I jumped up, ran off, found my friend Stephanie and asked her what to do. She told me that what had happened was normal. 'Oh, relax, it's just making out, Nina!' she said. 'Don't overreact.' She then directed me back to the waiting boy, to take up where we left off. Romantic, huh?

After The Kiss, I felt incredibly naive and inexperienced. The shocking realisation that people didn't always follow The Script as set out in movies left me second-guessing myself and wondering what the real hook-up rules were. In health class we had studied cross-section diagrams of male and female anatomy. I'd also read loads of 'Dolly Doctor' columns, which were mainly about icky discharges and how to protect yourself from STIs. None of this helped me understand this new world I was discovering or the mixed feelings I was having. Most of all, I was worried that if I admitted that I had no idea what 'the rules' were, I would appear inexperienced and clumsy (which I was).

It was years before I ever actually had sex. But what I took from these early fumblings was just how confusing it can be when you are trying to navigate your own and other people's desires and expectations.

Now, here's a secret. Guys are just as anxious as girls are about making out and sex. They might act all confident, as if they know what they want and what they are doing, but more often than not, they are just as worried about appearing inexperienced and 'bad at it' as girls are. Some boys turn to pornography to try to figure out what girls like. But this is rarely helpful since most mainstream pornography features actors who are paid money to act out unrealistic, over-the-top sexual fantasies that might actually cause injury, pain or distress if replicated in real life.

Another hurdle is all the confusing and contradictory messages girls receive about our bodies and sex. Have you noticed how girls are expected to walk an impossibly fine line where we must appear sexy but not *too* sexy, and available but not *too* available? (We are also expected to look both glamorous *and* effortlessly natural at the exact same time. Go figure.) What's worse, girls are told that in order to be valuable we must be desirable to others, but never act on any desires of our own, lest we be labelled a slut. And at the same time that we are meant to be vigilantly guarding our reputations, there is also pressure from friends and boys not to be too prudish or frigid, either.

Talk about pressure! No wonder so many girls feel judged and scrutinised. No wonder girls feel like their bodies and choices are being policed by others. And can you see how as long as we continue to judge girls in this way, none of us can really win? If we insist that girls look sexy and then shame them for it, or tell them not to have sex and then belittle them for being virgins, what is a girl supposed to do exactly?

There is also a nasty gender double standard at work here. Boys who are sexually experienced are often celebrated as heroes and studs while girls are called denigrating names like skank or slut. However, this doesn't mean that boys don't face other pressures. They might not be slut-shamed in quite the same way that girls are, but 'locker-room' culture places immense weight on boys to hook up with girls, and prove their girl-pulling power to other guys.

All of this pressure can transform sex into a battleground, with guys and girls pitted against each other as adversaries. When boys are encouraged to hunt down sex to boost their social status, and girls are taught to fend off sex to protect their reputations, hooking up becomes a contest of winners and losers, victors and victims. No wonder boys boast that they 'scored', as though sex is a game played against an opponent.

I also think it's incredibly revealing to look at the slang words we use to describe sex. Boys *nail*. They *bang*. They *hit it*. Sounds more like an excursion to the hardware store. Boys also *get lucky*, *get laid*, or *get action*. By contrast, girls are said to *give it up* or *put out*, as if sex is something they dispense rather than enjoy. And in romance novels the female characters *yield*, *submit* or *surrender*. In other words boys do, while girls get done. They get lucky, we just get screwed.

Talk about some sexist BS. Thankfully, we do not have to buy into such outdated nonsense. Which is just as well because who wants to share any sort of intimacy with someone they view as an opponent? And the good news is that most young people — boys as well as girls — genuinely want to have caring relationships and positive experiences around intimacy. So in this chapter I want to cut through all of the gender double standards and unhelpful cultural messages around sex and relationships, and talk instead about the issues that really matter, such as the issue of consent, the factors which eliminate a person's capacity to give consent, and your right to make choices around your body and sexuality. There is some confronting material in this chapter, but I know that most girls want honest information presented in an upfront way. So let's get started.

Yes means yes, no means no

Physical intimacy of any sort is supposed to feel good. Women want and enjoy sex as much as men and have the same sorts of urges and desires. But if you ever feel unsure, anxious, pressured or uneasy about something, this is a sign that things are moving too quickly for you. Remember, it's your body and your rules!

When it comes to hooking up and sex, it can sometimes feel as though there is a big grey area about what is and isn't consent. Where is the line exactly? This is a question that a lot of people struggle with because of various myths and misconceptions. So let's break it down:

- Sexual activity without consent is considered sexual assault, so consent is essential each and every time any sexual activity takes

place (this includes digital penetration and oral sex, not just intercourse).
- For a sexual act to be considered consensual, a person must agree to it *freely* and without any *pressure*, *force* or *coercion*. This means that a person needs to give their agreement eagerly and willingly, without any sort of manipulation, guilt or pressure.
- Consent must be *actively* given. This means that if someone freezes, goes stiff or silent, or does not say 'no', then they have not given consent. An absence of 'no' is not a 'yes'. As one educator once told me: don't settle for an unsure-sounding 'OK'. Hold out for an active, enthusiastic 'yes!'.
- For consent to be valid, a person must have the *capacity* to be able to give it. For instance, if someone is unconscious or asleep, or is heavily affected by drugs or alcohol, they cannot give consent because they lack 'capacity'. If someone engages in sexual activity with that person, this is sexual assault.
- In Australia, a person must be at least sixteen — or seventeen in South Australia and Tasmania — to legally consent to sexual activity.
- Consent can never be assumed. It must be given every time any sexual activity takes place — not just as a 'once off' at the beginning of

a relationship. This means that if a girl does something sexual with a partner once, she is not now obliged to do it again. Consent tonight is not consent tomorrow night.
- If a person consents to take part in one sexual act, such as oral sex, it does not mean he or she has consented to any other sexual act, such as penetrative intercourse. This also means that if a person receives oral sex, they are not obliged to then perform oral sex — or any other sexual act — in return.
- Consent is only valid for the person it was intended for.
- A person can withdraw his or her consent at *any time* during a sexual act. If a person changes his or her mind for any reason and no longer wants to continue, it is the responsibility of the other person to respect this and *stop*.
- The golden rule is that when negotiating any sort of sexual intimacy, both people have a responsibility to ensure that the other person is happy, enthusiastic, comfortable and consenting.

When I was in school, no-one taught us what consent was or how to communicate and 'check in' with the other person to make sure that both people are feeling happy, comfortable and consenting. I guess they figured we'd all just magically pick it up somehow. So don't feel embarrassed if you don't already know everything about negotiating consent. As a starting point, here are some helpful questions so that if or when you decide to be intimate with another person, you have some ideas of how to 'do' consent:

- 'What would you like?'
- 'Are you OK with this? Are you sure?'
- 'What do you want to do?'
- 'What feels good for you?'
- 'Do you want to slow things down?'
- 'Is everything all right?'

If in doubt, stop and ask. Remember, no-one is a mind reader. It can also be easy to misinterpret body language or other signals and expressions. For example, some people smile or giggle when they are happy. Other people do these things when they are nervous or uncomfortable. This means that physical cues can be unreliable and so some vocal interaction is necessary. The better both people are at speaking openly, the more likely they are to feel happy and comfortable about things. Here are some more tips on how to communicate how you are feeling:

Green light. If you feel comfortable, safe and happy and you want things to continue, some expressions that communicate you are feeling this way are:

- 'Yes. That feels good.'
- 'Yes. I like it when you do that.'
- 'Yes. Keep doing that.'

Yellow light. If you feel generally comfortable with what is occurring, but would prefer to move in a different direction, you could say:

- 'Instead of ... could we ...'
- 'I prefer it when ...'
- 'Could we try ...'

Red light. If you are in a situation where you do not feel comfortable, or are not sure what you want, it can be helpful to have some expressions prepared, such as:

- 'I'm not ready to do this. My answer is no.'
- 'I need you to listen to what I am saying and respect my decision. No.'
- 'I said no. I don't owe you an explanation.'
- 'Stop. I don't like it.'

Most importantly, remember that it is your body and your rules. You have the right to be respected.

Pressure points

When it comes to physical intimacy, there are different types of pressure that can make it difficult for a person to speak up and say that they feel that someone is crossing a line. It can be especially tough to speak up if you want to please someone or are anxious about losing their approval.

> My boyfriend told me that he had sex with his last girlfriend and that he wanted to have it with me. I felt embarrassed for not being as experienced and I really wanted him to like me. I was torn, though, because I didn't really want to, but at the same time, I didn't want to disappoint him or for him to break up with me, either. I think a lot of girls feel like this at some stage or another over sexual things. Torn between what is expected of us to do, what we feel obliged to do, and what we actually want to do.
>
> Lucy, 16

If a girl is pressured or coerced to engage in *any* sort of unwanted sexual activity, it is considered sexual assault, even if she had consensual sex with the person before. Most people who experience sexual assault know the person responsible. (You can find out more information and where to get help in Chapter 9 and at the back of this book.)

Just because someone likes a girl and is paying her attention, it doesn't mean she owes that person anything. If someone threatens to break up with you, gets angry or frustrated, uses guilt or pressure, or makes you feel as though your own feelings are wrong, that person is not respecting you or your boundaries.

> coercion: using pressure, guilt, power or manipulation to compel someone to do something they don't want to do

I recently spoke to a group of Year 10 girls who believed that if a guy got an erection while you were kissing him, it meant that you had 'excited him too much' and now it would be 'slack not to do something for him'. They honestly thought that they owed him some sort of sexual release. I told them that this is not true and reminded them that for consent to be valid, it has to be given freely and without any pressure or sense of obligation. Later, I asked a group of Year 10 boys what they thought and they agreed with me that girls do not 'owe' anyone sexual favours. Actually, did you know the average teen boy gets between five and ten erections *a day*? In fact, a teen boy can get an erection from just about anything, including the bouncing of a bus. Does this mean that the bus driver then owes him sex? Of course not!

Not long after this conversation, I sat down with some female university students to ask their opinions about what pressure can look like. What followed was a very honest conversation about the complex ways in which pressure can manifest and how power within relationships can sometimes be exploited. Their answers were very insightful and so I have decided to share some of them here so that you can better identify the different types of pressure that can contribute to sexual assault.

Verbal pressure: 'I thought you said you loved me.' Begging, flattering, name calling or arguing about sexual activity are types of verbal pressure which can reduce or eliminate a person's ability to give free consent. For example: 'You are just so hot, I can't help myself' / 'Why are you being so uptight about it? It's just sex.' / 'But you promised! Don't you love me?' / 'If I don't get it from you, I will get it from someone else' / 'I thought we agreed? You're not going to change your mind now, are you?' / 'You're killing me here'.

Power imbalance: 'He was the school captain and I was two grades below him. What was I supposed to do?' When one person is older, or has a lot more popularity or power than the other person, an unequal situation is created. This power imbalance can then contribute to the level of pressure felt by the person with less social status. The higher status person has a responsibility not to abuse their power.

Social context and expectations: 'It was his birthday. The hotel room was already booked. I didn't feel I could back out.' Sometimes pressure doesn't only come directly from the person instigating sex. Social context, expectations, and pressure from friends can also create or add to the pressure. For example, if a friend says, 'When are you going to hurry up and lose your V-plates? You're the last in our group!' / 'It's formal night! Everyone does it on formal night, it's tradition!', this can make a person feel as though they are obliged to have sex or do something sexual. This is not the case. Social pressure can be explicit or implicit, meaning that friends or partners don't necessarily have to say something directly in order for a person to feel pressure. Other examples might be the pressure a person feels because of a certain event such as a birthday, anniversary or other special occasion. Social pressure can also be exploited by a partner and this can undermine a person's ability to give free consent: 'All my friends are giving me crap about this! What's the big deal?' / 'Everyone expects us to have sex! It's my birthday.'

Emotional manipulation: 'He sulked until I gave in.' Emotional manipulation can include using guilt, sulking, ultimatums ('I'll break up with you if you don't'), pouting, the silent treatment or other strategies to make a person feel as though they have to do something sexual. It can also involve giving a girl gifts or paying for things like an expensive dinner as a way of trying to make her feel as though she 'owes' the other person sexual favours. This is coercion.

Drugs/alcohol: 'I agreed to a drink. Not to sex.' This includes drink spiking (putting alcohol or other drugs into someone's drink or food), getting someone deliberately drunk, or giving someone drugs or alcohol in order to lower their inhibitions and 'loosen them up'. It also includes using the fact that someone is already drunk to coerce them into sexual activity. Remember, a person who is heavily affected by drugs or alcohol does not have the capacity to give consent, making any subsequent sexual activity illegal.

Gender roles and cultural expectations: 'He thought I was playing hard to get. I wasn't.' Gender stereotypes and cultural beliefs can also contribute to sexual assault. For example, the belief that sex is a conquest, where men are the hunters and women are the prize, can make some boys feel entitled to pursue sexual activity with a girl, even if she has already said no. The belief that it is normal for girls to 'play hard to get' (and say 'no' when they really mean 'yes') is one of the most dangerous myths about sex, because it encourages boys to believe that not only is it OK to ignore what girls say, but that deep down, girls secretly want and expect this, too. By contrast, the stereotype that boys are 'always up for it' can put pressure on boys to feel obliged to do sexual things when they don't really want to. It can also teach girls to believe that boys should always be 'in the mood' and willing to be sexual. These stereotypes hurt *both* girls and boys and can make it difficult for individuals to express what their true boundaries are.

Non-neutral environments: 'I was in his car. He had all the control.' If a girl is on someone else's 'turf', such as in their car or bedroom, then that girl will often have less power in the situation compared to the person who 'owns' the space they are in. In sport we refer to this power difference as the 'home-ground advantage'. In sexual situations, being in an unfamiliar environment can often make a person feel more vulnerable and so the person with more power has a responsibility not to exploit the power imbalance.

Physical pressure: 'He was twice my size. It was intimidating.' Physical pressure involves using force, the threat of force, or other intimidation tactics to overpower someone. However, most girls are surprised to learn that the majority of sexual assaults do not involve physical force and that restraints are often psychological, not necessarily physical.

Say no to victim-blaming

If a girl is ever pressured or coerced into unwanted sexual activity, this is a crime and it is never her fault. It doesn't matter what she was wearing or doing. It doesn't matter if she was drunk or sober. It doesn't matter if she had dated or flirted with the person before. (Heck, I don't care if a person is doing naked cartwheels at 4 a.m. down Main Street — no-one has the right to touch a person without their consent!)

Unfortunately some members of society still hold attitudes and beliefs that imply that victims — and not perpetrators — are responsible for sexual violence. This is called victim-blaming and it is a way of shifting the responsibility and guilt off the perpetrator and onto the victim. When this happens, perpetrators can feel as though their actions are justifiable, while victims can feel isolated, unsupported and further distressed. This can then impact on their likelihood of reporting to police and seeking help to recover. Sexual assault has one of the lowest conviction rates of any crime. It is also the only crime where society continues to blame the victim instead of the offender.

But we can stop this by calling out victim-blaming attitudes when we hear them (such as attitudes that focus on a girl's dress or behaviour as a way of minimising the offender's responsibility) and by supporting survivors when they speak up. It takes a tremendous amount of courage for a survivor to speak up, so if someone ever discloses to you that they have experienced unwanted sexual behaviour, remember that this has taken a lot of bravery and that they must really trust you. (For more on how to support a friend, see Chapter 9.)

It's equally important not to blame girls who don't fight back when put in an uncomfortable or threatening situation. There are many reasons why a girl might freeze or go stiff and silent when she feels unsafe, unsure or uncomfortable. She might be scared that a person could turn violent if she confronts them. She might be in shock or feel powerless. She might feel anxious about hurting the other person's feelings or worried that they might get angry or reject her. She might feel embarrassed, confused, intimidated or distressed. All of these feelings are normal.

Girls are also not often taught *how* to speak up when they feel unsure or uncomfortable. For instance, when I was little I was told that it was never OK for someone to touch me in a way that made me feel uncomfortable. I was taught the proper names of my body parts and what sort of touching was normal and acceptable and what wasn't. But I was also taught to be nice to people. To not make a fuss or cause a scene. To make other people feel comfortable. To be accommodating and polite. And most importantly, to never overreact. Being accused of overreacting is something that a lot of girls are afraid of, because it implies we are hysterical and overly emotional. And somewhere along the way, the idea that girls were supposed to be polite and accommodating began to override the message that no-one was allowed to act in a way that made me feel uncomfortable.

I know that I am not alone. From a young age, many girls are taught to suppress their discomfort and smile sweetly when inside they are feeling uneasy. Like when they are told to sit on the lap of a creepy Santa Claus for a photo, or kiss a weird family friend, and their instincts say no but because an adult is telling them they should, they bite their tongue. Or when teen girls are on the bus and some creep gets a bit too close but they grin and bear it.

Can you see the problem? How can we expect girls to speak up when they feel uncomfortable if we have trained them from childhood to put other people's feelings ahead of their own needs? But while a girl might freeze for any one of these reasons, there is also a biological reason why people freeze and it is known as the fight, flight or freeze response.

The fight, flight or freeze response

Until recently, scientists believed in the 'fight or flight' survival mechanism. The idea was that when people were confronted with danger, their bodies would release a flood of adrenaline, which would give them the energy to either strike back against an opponent (fight) or run away and flee (flight). But scientists had only understood part of the story and they had left out the third, very common reaction that people have when they are scared: they freeze.

Think about animals in the wild. When in danger, some animals fight; they lash out against a threat, like a cat scratching at a dog. Some animals take flight; they dart quickly away and hide for cover, like a rabbit jumping into the bushes. And then there are those animals that freeze completely, like a deer in the headlights. People sometimes do that, too. When we see a dangerous snake in the wild, our first instinct is usually to freeze perfectly still in the hope that the danger may pass by without noticing us. We have evolved this way and the freeze response has been a core part of human survival for thousands of years.

But sometimes the freeze response kicks in when we don't really intend it to. It's not that a girl is a coward or that she is weak, it's that her body's first instinct is to freeze as a response to danger. I once spoke to a fifteen-year-old girl who had a guy sit next to her on the bus and put his hand up her skirt. She froze completely. At first she couldn't understand her reaction and she blamed herself. Once I explained the biological reasons behind freezing, she understood and immediately realised why she was not to blame at all.

It is important that we talk about this stuff so that you know not to blame yourself if your boundaries are ever crossed. And if it happens to another girl, you know not to blame her, either. Most of all, I want you to know that you have the right to assert yourself and control what happens with your own body. OK? OK.

Standing up, speaking out

Since girls aren't always taught how to speak up when they feel uncomfortable, I like to practise on little things in everyday settings. When someone sits uncomfortably close to me on public transport, I speak up and ask them to move over. When someone bumps into me on the street and they are at fault, I wait for them to apologise instead of immediately rushing in to assume the blame. And when a guy acts sleazy or inappropriate towards me, I call them out on it. ('Oh no you didn't!' *diva finger snap*)

Practising being assertive is a life skill that I think all girls should be taught. The point is not to be rude or aggressive, but confident, firm and self-assured.

Think of the tone of voice that a confident girl would adopt when sending back the wrong food order: calm, in control and direct. That's assertive communication. (Other tips: speak slowly and calmly, use a lower tone of voice, maintain eye contact, face the person straight on, don't be afraid to take up space.) Another skill I think we all need is how to speak up if you suspect that someone else may be in trouble. Remember, little actions can make a powerful and positive difference. This is called being an ethical bystander and anyone can develop ethical bystander skills.

If you suspect that another girl is in trouble, remember that she may be too scared to ask for help. So it's OK to take action to check if someone is all right or to be a circuit-breaker in the situation. You don't need to wait for someone to give you permission to say something. Just remember to keep yourself safe, too.

ethical bystander: a person who witnesses an unethical or threatening situation and who seeks to intervene in a safe, respectful way

For example, if you saw a girl from another school standing by herself at a bus stop, and a creepy guy was harassing her, you can be an ethical bystander by walking up to her and saying hi and sussing out if she is OK. This might feel odd since you don't know her, but I bet she will appreciate it. Or if you saw a girl being harassed online, you could report it, or send her a private message to see if she is OK.

Research shows that people are sometimes reluctant to speak up in such situations, not because they are indifferent or don't care, but because they worry that it's not their place to do something. Others will only intervene once they see that someone else has taken the initiative and intervened first. In fact, the more witnesses there are, the longer people wait to take action. This is called the bystander effect.

When I was sixteen, I was at a big house party where there were lots of teens from all different schools. A girl I didn't know from another school was sitting on a couch, looking as if she was about to pass out drunk. A super-creepy guy was all over her, and I could tell that she didn't like it but was too intoxicated to do anything. I looked around and thought, 'Where are her friends? Why isn't anyone doing anything to help her?' Without realising it, I was suffering from the bystander effect: I understood that there was a problem, but believed that it wasn't really my business and that someone else should be the one to take action.

Years later, I was in a similar situation in a nightclub. A guy was all over a girl who was really drunk, and it was obvious that she didn't want him around. I kept an eye on her for about five minutes and decided that the situation was getting worse, not better. So I walked past her and then casually asked, 'Hey, hon, do you know where the bathrooms are in this place?' My question was designed to be a circuit-breaker and it worked.

She immediately turned to me and said, 'Oh, they are over here. I need to go, too.' Once we were inside the bathroom, I could see the relief on her face. She phoned her friends, who had left the club. They came back and got her. It was a simple gesture on my part, but it made a big difference to her evening and I felt so much better knowing that she got home safely that night. Don't underestimate how powerful these small actions can be! (Plus, you always feel like a bit of a legend when you do a good deed for others. Good karma all around.)

Tips for being an ethical bystander
1. Suss out the situation. If you get a gut feeling that something is wrong, trust your instincts and try to read the situation to see what is happening. Is a person in need of help?
2. Next, ensure your own safety before taking further action. For example, if you see a person harassing a girl on a train station, you don't want to escalate the situation by confronting the aggressor directly, and becoming a target yourself. Consider what options are available to you and which is most likely to keep both you and the vulnerable girl safe.
3. Suss out who else is around. Are there other people who can assist you? One

option might be to involve other bystanders already present in the area. Alternatively, you could seek the help of an authority figure, for instance security personnel, a teacher, an adult or the police. In the above example the most effective thing might be to request the help of the station guard.

4. Take action. If no-one else is around or you decide to act immediately, weigh up what is your best option. It might be to interrupt, distract or remove the vulnerable person being targeted. Lend them your support. Remember, if you say to a distressed person, 'Are you OK?' they may say yes even if they are not, due to embarrassment, fear, uncertainty or confusion. So provide them with a concrete alternative option. For example, in the above situation, you could say to the girl, 'Hi, why don't you come over and sit with me and my friends for a while?'

5. Practice makes perfect. Sometimes we read a situation incorrectly and offer help when it's not needed. But there is absolutely nothing wrong with this and it's always better to be safe than sorry! Even if you offer help and it is not needed, this is still an extremely powerful gesture because it sends a strong message to the people around you that

you care about your community and that you want your community to be a safe, compassionate place.

Calling out casual sexism

Another awesome way in which girls can practise their assertiveness skills is calling out attitudes or jokes that cross a line for them. I bet that at some stage all of us have experienced what it is like to overhear a comment or joke that went that little bit too far. And when this happens it can be easy to tense up and go silent, can't it? Especially if we believe that the only reaction we will get will be: 'Oh, relax, it's just a joke. Stop taking everything so seriously, geez.'

I often speak to girls who are deeply troubled by racist, sexist or homophobic remarks that they overhear at school. Others feel equally distressed by fat-bashing or slut-shaming comments that their friends casually throw into conversation. It can be hard for girls to feel able to speak up in these situations, especially if they fear that other people might roll their eyes or tell them to lighten up. True? And sometimes girls find that when they try to speak up about issues which matter to them, they are dismissed or told to stop overreacting. In other words, 'Pipe down and back in your box, love! No-one needs to hear from you.'

I think the thing that bothers me most about this situation is that when we shut down a person's concerns we are only further entrenching the silence which allows offensive or discriminatory attitudes to exist in the first place. But you would be surprised how powerful it is to take a stand for what you believe in.

> *I used to find it really hard to speak up when someone made a sexist or homophobic joke. But then I realised that every time I did speak up, other people were secretly grateful because they were thinking and feeling the same way, too, but were too scared to act.*
> Sophie, 18

I love this comment from Sophie and can you see how it relates back to the bystander effect? Remember, when people feel awkward or uncomfortable (such as when they hear an offensive joke) they often wait to see if someone else will jump in first. So if you speak up, odds are that at least one person around you will feel relieved that you did! And if you see someone else speak up, keep in mind that it has probably taken a lot of guts for them to do that, so back them up.

There are other benefits to speaking up, too. Let's say that someone tells an offensive joke, such as a rape joke, at a party. If a person like Sophie chooses to speak up, this will do three things. First, it sends a message to any girl who has experienced sexual harassment or violence and lets her know that other people have her back. This can be hugely comforting. Second, it validates the feelings of everyone else who was also feeling uncomfortable and lets them know that they are not alone. Finally, it puts the joker on notice and lets them know that they are not necessarily in the majority. This might not sound all that impressive, but everyone present will be affected to some small degree. And this is exactly how we change culture: by degrees. So let's be each other's allies. Together we can make a powerful difference!

Quiz

Circle the answer that comes closest to describing your situation.

1. You are at a party and you notice that only the girls are being encouraged to drink from a certain container. One of the boys then jokes that it's got something 'special' in it. You:

A. Try some of the beverage. There is no way that you want to be left out of the fun!
B. Laugh it off. The boys are probably just being idiots.
C. Immediately address the situation. This sounds like drink spiking.

2. Your friend tells you that her boyfriend expects her to have sex with him after the school formal, but she doesn't want to. You:

A. Tell her that she should do it, otherwise he might dump her.
B. Change the conversation. This is up to her to figure out.

C. Tell her that it's not OK for him to use pressure like that and reassure her that if her gut is telling her it is wrong, then it's definitely not the right time.

3. You and your friends are discussing an exam that you just sat. One of your friends comments, 'I totally raped it!' You are shocked by the casual use of the word 'rape'. You:

A. Laugh along nervously, like everyone else.
B. Pretend as though you didn't hear it.
C. Calmly and assertively say that rape is not a trivial subject.

4. When a person feels threatened, scared or unsafe, they might:

A. Lash out and fight or run away and flee.
B. Freeze completely still.
C. Any of the above reactions are normal. This is called the fight, flight or freeze response.

5. It says on the news that a woman was sexually assaulted at a twenty-first birthday party that she was attending. A friend comments that the victim was probably drunk and asking for it. You:

A. Agree. Some women invite violence.
B. Stay silent.
C. Tell your friend that victim-blaming only excuses the actions of perpetrators and shames victims into silence. Not cool.

6. You are at a party when you overhear a boy bragging to his friends that he is out to get 'some action' that night. Later, you see him hanging around a girl who is slurring her speech and stumbling. He puts his arm around her and begins to walk off with her. You:

   A. Figure that if she doesn't want anything to happen with him, she will put the brakes on it.
   B. Mind your own business. This has nothing to do with you.
   C. Immediately follow after the couple, grabbing one of her friends for backup.

7. A good example of negotiation *without* pressure might be:

   A. Saying, 'What would you like to do? Are you sure?'
   B. Saying, 'What feels right for you? Do you want to slow things down?'
   C. Both of the above.

Now add up how many A's, B's and C's you circled, and check below.

Mostly A's

You're still figuring some of this stuff out and that's OK. We all start somewhere. But you might want to review the information on victim-blaming, consent and the different types of pressure.

Mostly B's

You're still working through some of these issues and don't always feel confident enough to speak up. That's OK as it can take some practice. You might want to review the information on being an ethical bystander.

Mostly C's

Well done! You have a strong sense of social justice and care deeply about the safety of the people around you. Keep it up.

Affirmations

I set my own boundaries and my own terms.

I control my own body and make my own choices.

I assert myself in a calm, confident manner.

CHAPTER 7

Healing heartbreak
by Danni

When I was sixteen, my first serious boyfriend broke up with me — and I was crushed. Why do they call it a crush when you first start liking someone? I would rename it a 'flutter', as that's how my stomach feels when I am infatuated. Crushed is how you feel when someone you adore tells you that they no longer want to be with you.

I can still recall the exact words he used and where he was standing. We were in my bedroom and he was holding my cuddly toy mouse. In hindsight, he was holding it up to place a barrier between me and him. He suspected I was going to explode right there in front of him, and he wanted to take cover (behind a rodent wearing a fetching gingham dress and a frilly bonnet, apparently).

And I cried. And I cried. And I cried.

Ms Mouse proved useless — for I did not explode, but rather, I imploded. My heart felt as though it was shrinking, not expanding. There was no anger, just despair. Darkness. Disbelief.

And then I had to go to school the next day and face everyone. I felt like everyone's eyes were on me — judging me. The one who got dumped. The Dumpee. The Big. Fat. Dumpling.

And you know what made it worse? Everyone telling me that I would or should get over it. That I would go on to have many more loves. (They were right.) That my heart would be broken many more times. (They were only partly right there. Yes, I have had heartbreak, but not as crushing as that first experience of rejection. Although I've loved others since then, and far more intensely, I had no understanding then that I would heal — no experience of heartbreak passing. I gained that knowledge through this first break-up.)

I became depressed afterwards. My school marks really suffered. I started binge drinking on weekends. I even played with dark thoughts about killing myself. I didn't really want to die; I just wanted to scare him into realising the mistake he'd made and come running back to me. The realisation that this was a manipulative, destructive fantasy added shame and humiliation to the mix of emotions already doing my head in. We girls aren't always very good at self-compassion, are we?

So here's the thing. I am not going to lie to you. If your heart is broken, it hurts. It is real. And it may well stay sore for some time.

This applies even if you are the one who did the breaking up. Making the decision that a relationship isn't working any more can be almost as heartbreaking as when someone breaks up with you. The sense of lost opportunities and dreams can leave you just as raw.

But no matter who initiated the break-up, it *will* get better. And not through drinking Breezers or playing make-up or break-up scenarios over and over in your head (or by calling and hanging up constantly, which I also did — thank God we didn't have Facebook and mobiles back then or I would have ended up with a one-way ticket to Stalkerville).

And you know what? Some of you may have just gone through a break-up and not felt anything like the pain I am describing here. The process of grief is a very personal journey and will look different for everyone. 'Some people might cry bucketloads, others barely a drop,' says psychologist Jacqui Manning, who sees a wide range of young women, and older women like me, at her relationship counselling practice. 'Whether you do or not doesn't mean you care more or less; it's just the way you are able to process your feelings at this moment.'

I asked Jacqui to explain for us the cycle of grief that people often go through when a relationship breaks up.

The grief cycle

There are some widely accepted stages of grief you may experience in the heartbreak time. However, these are just possibilities and they are not as neat and linear as some experts will have you believe. You may experience one or two of them, bounce through the last few and come right around to the first one again — it can be a bit of a merry-go-round!

Denial. In this stage of the grief cycle, your brain just can't accept that the relationship's over, and you are in a kind of shock. It's actually a protective mechanism for your heart and mind to have a bit of time to accept the news. Everybody spends different amounts of time here. It's a good idea to turn to your family and friends and debrief with them if you feel stuck here for too long.

Anger. When the reality hits, you may become furious at your ex for causing you pain or saying or doing hurtful things. Sometimes it can be beneficial to draw a line in the sand with your feelings and think of the things that make you angry with your ex, so you can reinforce why you don't want to go back to that relationship or why, in the big picture, the relationship's not good for you. Try not to make any big decisions at this time, though. Express the anger in healthy ways, such as through exercise, writing, drawing, music or having a good old pillow-punching session!

Bargaining. In this phase you think of ways to try to get your ex back or perhaps be friends. The bargaining may all be in your own mind — for example, 'If I get thinner, I'll get him back.'

Becoming friends with your ex soon after a break-up is really hard, because you once had romantic feelings for each other. I would strongly recommend you put some space and time in between your relationship and any potential friendship. This doesn't mean you will never be friends, but you need to allow your heart to heal. You will have the best chance to be true friends down the line if in the short term you avoid contact with each other — and that includes face-to-face, phone and Facebook contact and texting.

This may be impossible to do 100 per cent, as you might go to the same school or have the same friends, but ask a couple of your good girlfriends to be with you at parties or sit with you in class, and get them to remind you (several times if necessary!) that it's too early to be friends with your ex. Your heart is number one at this time, and it needs some time to lick its wounds.

Depression. This is when the sadness kicks in. It's a time for reflection (writing a diary may help) and taking time out alone and with your closest buddies for some nurturing. Resist the temptation to get drunk or high, as your physical self needs to heal from the shock also. Try to rest as much as possible and eat healthy food, even if you can only manage small portions. Remember, all you need to do is put one foot in front of the other. All healing involves taking two steps forward and one step back, so when you feel a setback, know that this happens to everyone and you just need to turn your focus back to what builds you up rather than tears you down. Maybe write down some words of personal power or draw a picture that reminds you that you are strong and will get through this, and stick it on your mirror where you will see it every day.

Acceptance. This is when you accept deep down that the relationship is over and perhaps that you may have contributed something to the break-up. You start to see the lessons in the situation. You are more able to think about your future and feel positive and hopeful that you will find someone else in time. You may still feel pain every now and then, but it is duller and not as frequent, and you are able to look forward more than you look backward.

I'm assuming you need support to move through the grief cycle, or you wouldn't be reading this chapter — fair enough? So here are my 6 Steps to Help Mend a Broken Heart.

Be careful not to dismiss these steps as unimportant or somewhat self-indulgent. I could have just as easily named this list the more impressive-sounding 6 Steps to Help Build Resilience.

Resilience is our ability to overcome adversity, to pick ourselves up when the going gets tough, and move forward. This ability is a vital life skill, as the only real certainty there is in life is that nothing is certain. And, as with all skills, resilience can be learnt and improved with practice.

So you, my darling, brave girl, are about to discover not only how to heal your heart but how to bounce back from any other trauma you may suffer throughout life. You are going to heal and develop your resilience, and in doing so, you will emerge from your experience of a break-up more hopeful and powerful. Promise.

Step 1: If you feel like crying, cry.

> This is a good sign, having a broken heart. It means we have tried for something.
> **Elizabeth Gilbert**[1]

Crying is a really important part of the healing process. Just weeks before I started writing this chapter, I broke up with my partner of almost three years, and I spent a solid two days in tears. I was quite committed to this! I cried with gusto and pride! I became an Olympic crier!

My tears felt pointless to me, but my dear friend Ella, who is a nurse, wrote to me to say I was actually doing vital work:

In nursing, we use normal saline for almost everything. Normal saline is the artificially made version of tears. We use normal saline for a lot of things, the two most striking to be to rehydrate patients (and believe me, when someone is acutely dehydrated they get a whole new lease on life once they're rehydrated) and to clean out wounds.

We use it to clean even the ickiest, most foul, most painful wounds (sometimes they're so messy we call them 'sloughy', and I don't even think I need to explain that: the word says it all). Even when it's infected and inflamed, normal saline — tears — clean out the wound. Salt acts as an antibiotic; it's effective at killing the germs quickly. Normal saline is the best way to clean out a wound because it gets rid of the crap and stimulates the healing process.

I was told some time ago that tears are the 'normal saline' for the wounds that we can't see. Just like a vial of normal saline will clean out a cut or a scratch, shedding tears helps heal our heart. It stings at first (as does cleaning out a wound) but when the pain is over, there's relief. Pain is our way of knowing something's wrong in our body, in our life. Healing from that pain takes time; it takes 'cleaning out' (with a lot of normal saline!); it takes life changes. Sometimes it means things need to stop for a little bit to allow them to change around.

I always consider tears to be the start of the healing process. Tears clean the wounds we cannot see, just like normal saline cleans out physical wounds.

Let the tears flow. Cleanse. Heal.

What if you're a non-crier? This doesn't necessarily mean you don't care — deeply. But there is a risk that you may be repressing your feelings of pain and that these will manifest elsewhere in your life later.

> Unexpressed emotions will never die. They are buried alive and will come forth later in uglier ways.
> **Sigmund Freud**

> *When I was completely broken once, I spent three weeks staring at the ceiling. I didn't cry. I stared. Silent. There was so much noise that I needed to make the world very small. The ceiling was the most interesting thing in the world to me. Sometimes we're too broken to cry, I think.*
> **Sarah Casey, postgraduate student**

It can be difficult if you are distraught after a break-up and yet your ex seems just fine, can't it? Perhaps you've even seen pictures of him out having fun with another girl. This will sting, but don't be fooled into thinking this means he didn't care about your relationship or that he's not suffering, too.

It might help you to hear a male perspective on why guys appear to get over break-ups faster than girls, from the writer Yashar Ali:

> Women often wonder: How can these men move on so quickly with another woman? How can they not feel crazy like me? Why am I the one who texts, calls and emails him? Has he forgotten what we shared? Did he ever care? ...
>
> A man's sense of emotional expression may be different, but the way he thinks and feels are not. They are often struggling with heartbreak every bit as much as women ...
>
> The difference with men is that they don't share their heartache — they don't talk about it. Their issue goes back to the way in which men in our culture are stifled, emotionally trapped by their conditioning. Their focus is to hide any visible sign of weakness, emotional fragility and vulnerability. It's the ultimate insult for a man to appear emotional, to be seen as 'a pussy'.[2]

Instead of working through his grief and allowing himself to feel pain, Ali argues, a guy is more likely to express his pain through raw anger (by yelling at you or treating you like you are now his enemy) or by remaining silent (simply ignoring you and seeming to want to have nothing more to do with you). He concludes:

> But it's ultimately sad, because while you grow stronger, driving through the pain, he has dismissed it and it's just going to haunt him again, again and again. That detour he took? It comes at a high price.

Yep. Although it is tempting to repress pain by distracting ourselves or refusing to tune in to our sadder feelings, that is when the pain may get 'stuck' and be unhelpful. For girls and boys.

Feelings are not good or bad; they just are what they are. Grief, anger and anxiety are all important emotions to experience,

> repress: to suppress or reject thoughts, feelings or memories

and we need them for guidance. For example, if someone is treating you badly and you feel angry about it, anger is giving you the message that it's not OK for someone to treat you that way. Think of your heart as a bus, and your emotions as the passengers. Allow the whole spectrum of emotions on your bus — that is, don't kick anyone off — but don't let anger or anxiety hop in the driver's seat (at least, not for long!).

In *The Gifts of Imperfection*, Brené Brown talks about the fact that when we numb the Dark, we also inevitably numb the Light.[3] In other words, if we try to hide from our darker emotions such as fear, disconnection, shame and vulnerability, we also limit our capacity to feel joy, gratitude and grace. This makes sense, doesn't it?

It's important to let ourselves experience the full range of human emotions so we can become wholehearted girls and women.

Wallow in sorrow if that's what helps you to express, rather than repress, your grief. You might be able to do this through listening to sad music or watching heartbreaking movies. When she was thirteen, my daughter, Teyah, had a playlist on her iPod entitled 'Depressing Songs'. (I am assuming they are sad songs about unrequited love, not just truly crapola songs.) My personal favourite tear-jerker is the song 'Torn'. If films are more your thing, watch movies about great lost loves.

Even if you cannot, or do not want to, scream out or cry, do not engage in other dangerous methods of coping with dark emotions, such as self-harming. I mention this because, in my experience working with young women, self-harming is alarmingly common.

> Content warning: Before you read any further, we want to give you a heads-up that this is a discussion of self-harm that may trigger a strong emotional response in some readers.

Self-harm is when a girl purposely injures herself, usually in secret. She might do this by cutting, burning, biting or branding her skin. She may hit herself or bang her head, pull her hair out, pick and pull at her skin, or pick at old sores to open them up again.

When a girl who fears expressing her rage and sadness to the world self-harms, she may feel as though she is releasing pent-up steam, as if opening the valve on a pressure cooker. The act may bring a temporary sense of relief. Some girls who are numbed by depression or trauma tell me that self-harming is a way to feel something again.

A girl who doesn't know who, or how, to ask for help may be using her injured body to send a message. There are girls who self-harm because they feel that they are not in control of aspects of their life. And when a relationship unexpectedly breaks up, it can feel as though things are temporarily out of your hands, can't it? For some girls, self-harm may be a way of seeming to gain control.

But self-harm brings with it guilt, depression, self-loathing, anger, fear and isolation from friends and family. It is not helpful long term and carries the risk of serious health hazards, including scarring, infection and damage to nerve endings.

If you feel tempted to do something like this, seek help and support. The underlying reasons you feel the need to self-harm should be uncovered and worked through with a professional, who will also help you to develop healthier ways of identifying, coping with and expressing painful emotions. Communication is key. In Step 4, I discuss the value of talking to people, and I give advice on whom to speak to and how to talk about painful experiences. Let these pointers guide you to making the connections you need so that you can move forward.

In the short term, try these alternatives: count to ten or wait fifteen minutes, to give the feeling a chance to pass. Say, 'No!' or 'Stop!' Try relaxation techniques such as yoga, or go for a run or do some other kind of hard physical exercise. Another accepted temporary solution is to choose an alternative, such as squeezing ice cubes between your fingers until they go numb, eating a chilli, standing under a cold shower or drawing in red on your body instead of cutting.

Step 2: Be kind to you.
Eat chocolate. Drink soothing cups of tea. (Chamomile tea soothes me, as do Caramello Koalas.) Wear comfy, loose clothes and ugg boots (or as a friend calls them, 'hug boots' — I love the idea of them being sheepskin hugs for your feet). Do whatever it takes to feel nurtured.

When my kids are sick, I make them 'nests'. Basically, this involves fluffing up their doonas and piling pillows on the lounge, tucking them into this nest, and bringing them trays piled with food and drinks with those bendy straws that allow you to sip without even lifting your head. Somehow all this paraphernalia is really helpful, isn't it? So make yourself a little nest. A Nest for the Broken-hearted. Put a sign up: 'Shhh ... Healing at work'.

Be kind to yourself in other ways, too. Monitor your self-talk closely. Silence your inner critic if you find you are saying things to yourself like 'You are such a loser!' or 'Of course it failed, you're a failure at relationships!' Replace these unhelpful thoughts with positive affirmations such as the ones at the end of this chapter. A useful guide to monitoring your self-talk is to ask yourself, 'Would I say this to a friend in her hour of need?' If the answer is no, then don't bully yourself, either!

I know it can be hard to get that insistent voice out of your head, but there are some practical techniques that can help. Imagine that your negative self-talk is floating above your head in a speech bubble, like in a cartoon. As your self-talk nags on, watch the speech bubble crumble into black dust. You can also try picturing your negative self-talk as just 'blah, blah, blah', to take away its power.[4]

At times of great vulnerability, we need to also watch how we care for ourselves physically. Did you know that sunlight increases your vitamin D level, which can reduce your risk of depression? According to the team at Reach Out, an excellent resource for teens on all things related to mental health, by boosting your vitamin D, you're increasing your level of the hormone serotonin, which affects mood and alertness and is the target of many antidepressants. Make some time to sit in the sun or go for a walk outside.

This is also a wonderful time to begin engaging in a relaxation method. Try meditation or creative visualisation (we do these with girls in schools and they always find them blissful), get a massage, relax in the bath, try Pilates or yoga, or burn calming and stress-relieving essential oils such as lavender, cinnamon, orange or myrrh. Learn what most nurtures you.

Step 3: Now stop crying and get up!
Right. You've had your wallow time. Some of us need one or two days, others a little longer — but you have

to start moving again now or you will get entrenched in nest land. You may never get out — and you don't want to be wearing hug boots and sipping out of bendy straws forever, do you?

Don't feel like moving yet?

Fake it until you make it.

In other words, even though you might not *feel* like getting on with things yet, start channelling all that sad somewhere. Walk. Out of the lounge room. Out the front door. Hell, go for a run if you'd like to! After my marriage broke up, I started running. I had never been a runner, yet I just put on my tunes and started pounding it out on the treadmill. And in no time at all, I was running 10 kilometres. Like a boss. It made me feel strong and in control.

Today as I write I am recovering from a terrible flu. It had left me cold and broken on the floor. OK, OK, those words might actually be inspired by the song 'Torn', but the cold really did leave me physically wiped out. I think all the sad emotions I had over my recent break-up compounded this bug and really floored me. And of course, being so sick and vulnerable meant I missed my ex-boyfriend very much. So my freshly healed 'love bites' (see what I did there? I was bitten by love) opened up, too. I became a mass of tears, snot and phlegm.

But after three days of me being bedridden and surviving on nothing but mandarins and Minties (for oral freshness), a very good mate took me to task and staged an intervention. He wrote:

> *Danni, enough moping. You know as well as I do, it's time to get up and make some positive moves. Start to treat yourself like a 'treat'! And turn off that bloody sad music! Go eat something that doesn't start with M! Get dressed! GO, GIRL.*

How lovely is Aaron? And how right!

So my plan for the day is to write some more on this chapter (because golly it's helping me — I hope it's helping you, too), then I am going to get a pedicure and take myself off to the movies. This girl is bouncing back! With shiny toes!

It's going to be a better day. Fact.

So stop the eternal shuffle of emo songs on your iPod and trade the soppy movies for funny ones. Laughter is incredibly healing, so no matter how dark things have been, open yourself up to the idea of seeing the funny side of things again. Yes, even your break-up. You may find that, like me, once you allow a little humour back into your life — and even poke fun at yourself a bit — the intensity of your most painful emotions will begin to fade.

Step 4: Talk to someone.

It's vital to make careful choices about whom you turn to for compassion. You don't want to reveal your sadness and shame to someone who is going to respond in such a horrified way that you end up feeling as though you need to make them feel better.

Nor do you want to confide in someone who will offer sympathy ('Poor you!') but not empathy ('I understand; I have felt that way before, too'); the friend who feels so uncomfortable with your vulnerability that he or she goes on the attack ('How did you stuff that up?' or 'That guy was always a jerk — let's get him!'); the friend who refuses to acknowledge that you actually can make mistakes, too ('You were totally in the right — you're perfect!'); or the friend who just wants to compete in the sad stakes ('Oh, that's not so bad. Remember when I broke up with John? That *was* devastating').

We should look for compassion from 'someone who is deeply rooted, able to bend, and most of all … someone who embraces us for our strengths and struggles'.[5]

In other words, share your feelings with someone who has earned the right to share in them.

> When I was dumped by what was then 'the love of my life', I thought it was absolutely the end of the world for me, and as dramatic as it sounds, I felt like I was worthless and useless and that I now had nothing else going for me in life. As soon as it happened I put on every sad song I could find in my 'depressing/sleepy-time songs' playlist and bawled my eyes out for a good three hours. I took the day off school because I couldn't bear the thought of facing anyone and having to face the embarrassment of

being dumped. I mean, no girl wants to say they got dumped. The person who was there for me the most was my mum. She cried with me and said, 'Oh, darling, if I could take away your pain I would.' I think it is important to have a good relationship with someone you can confide in, whether it is your mum, dad, aunty, uncle or even a close friend.

Melanie, 18

You may want to consider seeing someone such as a counsellor or psychologist for more specialised support if three or more of the following apply to you:

- The break-up was a complete shock for you.
- You see your ex everywhere (school, uni, work, parties, etc.).
- Your ex was the one who broke up with you.
- You feel as though your ex was your only friend or provider of support.
- You don't have other friends or family around you.
- You have considered hurting yourself.
- You feel your relationship defined how you feel about yourself.
- You feel hopeless about your future — relationships or otherwise.
- Your ex has moved on with someone else and you can't stop thinking about it.
- You think all relationships are negative.

- You are turning to unhealthy coping mechanisms, such as alcohol or drugs or self-harm.
- You are not coping with school, study or work, and are finding excuses for days off.

If you don't know where to look for a counsellor or psychologist, ask your local GP for a referral.

At various points in my life I have seen a psychologist for extra support. I highly recommend doing so. It is not in the least bit scary — rather, I think of talking to a psychologist as a treat. It's a little like going for a mind massage! How often do you get the opportunity to sit down and discuss yourself for an hour — without the need to even ask the other person how they are? Me time!

Step 5: Don't play at regrets.

> She could never go back and make some of the details pretty. All she could do was move forward and make the whole beautiful.
> **Terri St Cloud**[6]

'I wish I hadn't said that really stupid thing to him/called him so many times and made him feel smothered/got jealous every time he talked to another girl ...'

Stop. You can't turn back time, so all this wishful thinking is not constructive. Plus, cut yourself some slack! Those things you think you did wrong are all part of learning. Making mistakes is normal and we all do it. And now is the best time to learn, as the stakes aren't usually quite as high as when you're older and married with ten kids, perhaps (although the stakes may feel huge right now, I know).

> There is nothing worse than giving everything you have to a guy, and then without reason he ends it. After what I thought were the best few months I have ever had with a guy, at recess at school he came and he ended it. No reason, out of the blue. For a girl, giving yourself to a guy in different ways is a big thing. This boy was my first for a lot of things, and I trusted him completely. When he ended it, I was devastated. I couldn't stop crying. And you continuously think to yourself, 'Why me? Why am I not good enough? What is wrong with me?' Over time, though, things do get better. I always looked to this quote and it always changed my point of view: 'Breaking up is not a stupid thing. Instead, it makes you a better person and realise your mistakes.'
>
> Mady, 16

> In future, something I probably wouldn't do again would be messaging him about five hours later saying, 'I can't do this.' I mean, come on, I AM AN AMAZON WOMAN, I AM STRONG, I DON'T NEED YOU. YOUR LOSS, NOT MINE. SO

> *LONG, SEE YA LATER, GOODBYE, AU REVOIR. You can't dwell on the past and you definitely can't change how someone feels; you have to move forward. My first heartbreak has taught me to be strong and to not settle for second best, and to know what I want and strive to get it — however, this has also made me pick the littlest things out when trying to find a new boyfriend, aka, I'm way too fussy.*
>
> Melanie, 18

Rather than dwelling on the mistakes of the past, think about what you have learnt that might help you in moving forward. Begin finding answers to these key questions: what have I learnt about me and what I need in a relationship? What type of partner am I looking for?

Investing time in thinking about your responses can be really helpful. I believe that if we don't learn from the past, we tend to go on to simply repeat the same patterns again and again until we get it!

I realised after my recent break-up that although I had been madly, crazily in love, to be truly happy long term I needed a partner who could be there to work equally with me on our family. So what type of man did I first get asked out on a date by? A man who came with limited time to see me and a range of complications on the home front that ensured he would need lots of my support. What did I do?

Fortunately, I saw that history was repeating itself just to check whether I was a fast or slow learner (OK, OK, a few close girlfriends also may have had to highlight the lesson for me) and I stepped back before getting involved.

In my recent break-up, I was the one who decided that the relationship was not working and needed to end. And here's something I can tell you from the heart: regret may also rear its head when you initiate the split.

As you find yourself single again, all of your ex's good qualities — the ones that attracted you in the first place — may suddenly blow up to gigantic proportions in your mind. Meanwhile you might go completely blank when you try to remember all those valid reasons you had for breaking up. And then suddenly all the happy times may start replaying themselves in your brain, like a flashback scene in a movie stuck on an endless loop. You must have been in the grip of temporary madness when you decided to break up, right? No! Put down the phone. Cancel that Facebook message you're halfway through writing to your ex. Look at videos of adorably naughty puppies instead. Or kittens if you insist.

Remember that even when it was you who made the decision to split, you may be going through the process of grief. You had hopes and dreams in the early days of the relationship, but for whatever reason, they didn't become reality. That can be heartbreaking. But don't let the heartbreak fool you into thinking that the only way you will feel happy again is to call up your ex and say it was all a horrible mistake and you didn't really mean it and can you just go back to how it was before and pretend it never happened …

Take a breath and put the whole situation into perspective. Yes, there were probably good things about the relationship and good qualities in your ex, and you should celebrate and honour those. But it's just as important to honour the reasons that made you decide to end the relationship, and to be protective and nurturing of your long-term happiness.

> I was dating someone who was a nice guy — just not the right guy for me. We were on different wavelengths about too many things, so we didn't really 'get' each other. When I stopped seeing him, close friends said I was crazy (mainly because they thought he was really hot, which is never a good enough reason on its own to go out with someone!). What was actually crazy was that I then regretted rejecting this guy. I felt miserable for a while and had moments where I blamed myself, as though there must have been something wrong with me for not being able to make a relationship work with someone who everyone else thought was hot.

Vanessa, 19

CREATE YOUR OWN LIFE LINE

When a relationship ends, it's easy to fall into the trap of thinking that just because this endeavour didn't work out as you hoped, somehow your whole life is a mess. A great way to gain perspective is to zoom out and look at the overall storyline of your life. That's where creating your own life line comes in. It's like one of those time lines you do in history — only cooler, because it records *your* life ... and beyond.

1. Get the biggest piece of paper or cardboard you can find. Join a couple of sheets together with sticky tape if necessary. You need enough room to record all the big milestones of your life.
2. Draw your life line on it. It can be a straight line stretching across the width of the sheet, a winding path that meanders across the page, a diagonal line from one corner of the sheet to the opposite corner — whatever works for you.
3. At one end of the line, draw a dot and write your birth date.
4. Next, estimate how long you will live. This might feel a bit weird, because it means facing up to the fact that, like everyone, you won't be here forever. Pick an age, but don't get too hung up on the number. It's not as though by writing it down you will be setting the time of your demise (this is a powerful exercise, but it's not *that* powerful!). Draw a dot and write down the age. Don't put the dot right at the end of your life line. Leave a little room for events that will happen after you are gone.

5. Work out where today sits on your life line, make a dot there and write down the date.
6. Between your birth date and today's date, add major events to your life line, such as starting preschool, primary school and high school; learning to ride a bike; getting the mumps; the birth of a brother or sister; the death of a grandparent; a big academic or sporting achievement or setback; first kiss; first break-up. Record everything significant that has happened to you or that you have done, whether it made you happy or sad.
7. Now it gets exciting. Imagine big things you will do and experience in the future. What are your hopes, dreams and goals? Put dots on your life line approximately when these might take place, and write down each event. Every girl will have a different set of future events on her life line — for instance, complete a university degree, get a job, start a business, travel overseas, become fluent in another language, do volunteer work for a great cause, commit to a long-term relationship, start a family and so on.
8. Now imagine your legacy to the world and add events that will take place after you have gone. For instance, if you added children to your life line, think of the things they will do and experience when you are no longer

around. What about any organisations that you worked for and the community you contributed to — how might your actions influence them in the future?
9. Let your inner artist or crafty girl go wild if you want. Draw pictures representing the events on your life line, or make a collage by adding images from magazines. Add colour or glitter and decorate the page to make it truly yours.
10. Now sit back and take a look at all the things you have experienced and will experience, all the ups and downs, the setbacks you have had, and all the goals you will achieve. When you see your life from this angle, does it change your perspective on heartbreak? Can you see how one relationship break-up, while painful and requiring time to heal, is not representative of your whole life? How do you feel when you think about all the incredible things you will do and create in your time here on earth?

Step 6: Forgive.

While forgiveness is one of the most challenging stages in the healing process, it is critical. The best approach to finding forgiveness is to focus on healing yourself rather than focusing on your ex. The key is 'letting go of the power the other has over us, by forgiving them and letting ... go', according to Melinda Phillips, of Good Grief, an organisation that helps people going through change, loss and grief. Once you forgive and let go, you will be able to move forward.

This makes sense, doesn't it — but how do we achieve this?

1. **Detox.** First try to actively release feelings of anger, hurt and rage from your body and mind — punch some cushions while thinking of your ex, scream almightily in a private place, go for a run, cry, write a brutally honest letter telling your ex how hurt and angry you are (and then burn it), make a list of all the reasons you're glad you're not with your ex any more.
2. **Reflect.** Have a think about what forgiveness is. Forgiveness is not excusing bad treatment or giving others permission to treat you badly. It is about letting toxic feelings of resentment and bitterness out of your system so you can heal and allow positive emotions to return. If you have constant intense negative thoughts about the past, it is likely that these will block positive emotions such as joy, contentment and optimism. If you start letting go of anger or thoughts of getting even, you'll be able to create a future rather than staying stuck in the past.

3. **Accept.** Some say forgiveness is the giving up of all hopes for a better past. To create a better future there needs to be some level of acceptance about the situation as it is, so you can think about how to move forward rather than remain stuck feeling sad, angry or hurt that the situation happened in the first place. Say to yourself something like 'This isn't how I expected or hoped it would be, but it is. Now, what is one thing I can do today to build my positive future?' And take it day by day, putting one foot in front of the other until you're running again!
4. **Change perspective.** No person is all good or all bad, and even though your ex might have behaved badly, there was something good about your ex that attracted you in the first place. Try to remind yourself that everyone (including you!) is usually doing the best they can with the resources and life's lessons they currently have. Your ex's best has certainly not been good enough for you and doesn't live up to what you want from a relationship, so welcome the fact that you've learnt this sooner rather than later, leaving you free to find a partner who better matches your relationship values and how you want to be treated.

Write down a list of all the things you would love in a future partner. You might find that your ex had some of the attributes you're looking for, but there were certainly things your ex was lacking. Rather than feeling sad you're not with your ex any more, acknowledge your ex's good points and know that you're going to find a new, improved, 'plus' version of that person sometime soon![7]

> OK — so the forgiveness thing. I let myself get all emotional, then I went to a park near the river and wrote down on a piece of paper all the things I forgave my ex-boyfriend for. I forgave him for his attachment to his mother, for his yuck head space ... for his weakness with not being able to 'be' with me ... After I'd finished writing everything down, I went down to the river and put it in the water and watched it float downstream until the water swallowed it. It was very healing. I had my iPod with me and after I'd 'released' all of that energy, I just started dancing, then jumped onto a table and continued to dance until people were giving me strange looks. :) The only way to get through something like this is forgiveness, but at the beginning, you need sad movies, bad poetry, depressing music, chocolate and some time alone. Forgiveness takes its sweet time, but I got there.

Carly Jay Metcalfe, poet

Healing overall may take its own sweet time, but you will get there.

PS Don't be too hard on yourself if you make mistakes along the way. Reading back over this chapter six months after writing it, I will admit that during the course of trying to heal my heart I did a number of the things I advise here not to do. Sending heartbroken texts? Check. Sending emails that tried to get my ex to remember the good we had rather than being angry towards me? Check! Check!

Some days I feel powerful and have clarity; other days I am a little more wobbly. Rather than getting too disappointed with myself when I fail to follow the 6 Steps to Help Mend a Broken Heart, I choose to be compassionate to myself. I choose to accept that I have a big heart so it takes effort to heal it.

You, too, may find the journey challenging, and there may be setbacks.

Be kind to yourself. Review the steps. Take baby steps towards them if that's all you can manage, knowing that at least, for the most part, you're heading in the right direction. And know this: you will be OK. As all pain does, this, too, shall pass. xx

Quiz

Circle the answer that comes closest to describing your situation.

1. What have you done with your ex's mobile phone number?

- A. Pressed delete. Hard.
- B. Saved it so if your ex should ever call you, your ex's caller ID will come up. You prefer to know who's calling you so you can make a sensible decision on whether to answer or not.
- C. Saved it because you are still texting your ex daily.

2. Your girlfriends invite you out a week after your break-up. What do you do?

- A. Accept and dress really hot in case you run into your ex.
- B. Accept because it's good to keep busy, and being with people who love you will be healing.
- C. Say no because you do not want to leave the house yet. Besides, that would mean getting out of your PJs.

3. There is a party this weekend that you and your ex were both invited to before you split. What do you do?

- A. Go to the party and flirt up a storm in front of him so he can see what he's missing out on.

B. Go to the party and make sure you take a close friend with you for moral support.
C. Decide it's too soon and stay home alone. In your PJs. Crying. Again.

4. A month after you and your ex broke up, you feel:

A. Amazing and thankful your ex is no longer a part of your life.
B. Good and relatively happy. You've even had a day or two where your ex wasn't the most present thing on your mind.
C. Hopeful, because you heard from a friend that your ex may be thinking about coming back to you.

5. The thought of kissing someone other than your ex is:

A. Fantastic, as you can then make sure your ex finds out all about it.
B. Exciting, and quite possible in the near future.
C. Impossible, as you're fairly certain no-one else will ever love you.

6. What do you do with all the pictures of your ex on your Facebook page?

A. Delete them. You also 'unfriend' him and his friends and family.
B. Nothing. They're part of your history.
C. Stare at them for hours. And then go over to his page and Facebook-stalk him.

7. What do you do on your ex's birthday?

- A. You can't remember the exact date and don't really care!
- B. You write a standard 'happy birthday' message on his Facebook wall, as you figure you may as well keep things friendly.
- C. You meet up with him and bring gifts to try to win him back.

Now add up how many A's, B's and C's you circled, and check below.

Mostly A's

You like to think you are over your ex — but are you really? The opposite of love is not hate; it's indifference. It seems that you are still emotionally connected to your ex through anger, resentment and a desire for revenge. This may not be healthy for you long term. And it will make it more challenging for you to connect with new people. It would be helpful for you to find someone whom you can share your pain with and who can support you. Also try to work through the forgiveness activities given earlier.

Mostly B's

You seem to have a healthy sense of perspective and are taking sensible steps towards caring for yourself during this stage. Go, you!

Mostly C's

Things are still very tough, aren't they? But you need to be kind to yourself and seek some extra support on the journey so you can move beyond Step 1 of the 6 Steps to Help Mend a Broken Heart. Make today the day you seek support.

Affirmations

I give myself permission to heal.

I am loveable and can give love.

I can control only myself and my own reactions.

CHAPTER 8

Single? In a relationship? Who cares? I'm awesome!

by Danni

> Every depressing sensation you can feel as a single person — misunderstood, isolated, and sad — you can certainly feel while in a relationship. And the elations you feel in a relationship — satisfied, triumphant, and ecstatic — you can feel while being single.
> **Samara O'Shea**[1]

There is absolutely nothing wrong with wanting to love and be loved. In fact, I think being in the right relationship is one of life's greatest joys, and when I am truly connected to the right man, my heart sings. However, I do think our hearts can sing amazing solos as well and that sometimes we fall into the trap of thinking we will only be happy if we are one of two.

In this chapter, I want to help you deconstruct that idea. The goal is not to turn you off wanting a partner, but rather to help you realise you'll be OK with or without one.

But for now, let me confess that I have a long-standing love affair with ... love.

When I was fourteen, I kept a diary. Called 'My Sweet Dreams', it was part of a range of merchandise that went with a popular teen romance book series, which I avidly read. The titles of the books included *The Summer Jenny Fell in Love*, *Portrait of Love*, *First Love*, *Forbidden Love* and *Love, Love and More LOVE!* OK, OK, I made that last one up — but you get the idea, right? The formula was this: young girl (usually smart and not particularly popular) gets swooped upon by a very hot, kind-hearted, funny guy. And they fall in love. Hard and fast. It was delicious! Irresistible! And I wanted a piece of this love action.

The diary was structured with goals for each month. Mine are best summed up by what I wrote for July:

> To meet some boys and to be more popular. I love, love, love boys! But none like me! And I am scared of them! Problem!

And each month I seemed to fall in 'love, love and more LOVE' with someone different. Craig. Stephen. Terry. Even a guy intriguingly named Foxy. Or, rather, I fell in love with *the idea of being loved by them* and the possibility that I could, finally, be partnered up. In reality, I hardly spoke to any of them, for I was shy around males at that stage in my life. Yet despite the lack of real-world contact, all these boys had a place in my desperate and dateless heart; all were seen as possible *solutions*.

To me, being single seemed like a condition that I needed to be cured of. What is wrong with me? I wondered. Why doesn't a boy 'discover' smart and not particularly popular Danni? When was my real life, my love life, going to begin? Future boyfriend — hurry up already!

It is not just the novels we read as teens that would have us think singledom is for losers. What about all those romantic comedies we watch, which are really all about curing the solo disease? Meanwhile the magazines we buy also taunt us with the glossy lives of celebrities in love. In Hollywood it seems that when two celebrities pair up, they actually begin morphing into each other and become a whole new super-celebrity entity. And when they break up, it's shocking. My teen daughter, Teyah, wept when one of her boy-band crushes broke up with his girlfriend. 'But Mum, they were perfection!' she wailed.

Yes, we do get led into believing those cute, cute couples are living a life more shiny than ours. And we feel devastated when they split, assuming they will no longer be happy or whole. A broken whole. Now just half a shattered heart.

I also blame love songs for our hopeless romanticism. It's easy to feel left out when you haven't experienced anything like the lyrics you find yourself singing along to, isn't it? Even if the songs deal with heartbreak, at least there was love there to begin with, right? Ever heard ''Tis better to have loved and lost, than never to have loved at all'? That line from a poem by Tennyson really resonated with me as a teen girl. I remember thinking I would give anything to have someone miss me so much that they had to put their loss in a poem or a song. What could be more romantic?

And there are very few songs that celebrate a woman being single. Even Beyoncé's 'Single Ladies' were only single because he hadn't chosen to propose — not because they were just having far too fabulous a time to *want* any man to propose!

Meanwhile popular TV shows that pit women against each other to win a marriage proposal from a bachelor perpetuate the myth that men are scarce prizes and we must compete with one another to win them.

But the message that being single is for losers or just a stage before life really begins with a partner starts working away at our subconscious before the teen years. It started way back when we were little girls.

Let's take a moment to deconstruct some of the fairy tales we were told, because I think we are still haunted by some of their messages.

Princess myths

When you were a little girl, how many princesses did you ever read about who were happy rocking the kingdom solo? None. Single princesses are usually desperately lonely and unloved — think Cinderella scouring the floors, Rapunzel locked up in a tower.

Often the princess, or would-be princess, is at risk of harm and is being treated cruelly, usually by jealous older women — so much for celebrating the sisterhood. She needs a man to rescue her. Not just any man — he must be handsome and wealthy. Any women she does have close to her are either ugly (Cinderella's stepsisters), old (Fairy Godmother types) or ugly and old (wicked witches). It seems no princess or princess-wannabe in her right mind would risk female competition!

In most fairy tales, particularly the Disney versions, often the girl's only friends during the awkward pre-him time are woodland animals such as birds and squirrels. In Ariel's case, it's sea creatures. In Belle's, it's cutlery. A girl has to make do in lonely ol' single town. Perhaps these characters are the childhood version of the adult stereotype of the lonely, crazy cat lady — a stereotype that would have us believe that if we don't get a partner, all we have to look forward to is a future filled with felines.

Often the princess will do anything to be noticed and loved. The little mermaid was prepared to cut off her fins and give up her enchanted voice just so a guy would notice her. (And PS, in the traditional telling of the tale, the prince takes quite a shine to the little mermaid but he's all preoccupied trying to track down a beautiful girl who saved him from drowning in a shipwreck. Because the little mermaid no longer has a voice, she's unable to explain to him that, hey, that girl is *her*. So the prince ends up falling in love and marrying the wrong girl. And the little mermaid dies. Happily. Ever. After.)

There are so many stories featuring beautiful young girls who are prepared to kiss frogs or put up with beastly behaviour for years in the hope they will eventually turn some jerk into a prince. It's revealing, too, that in all the transformation tales, it is the beautiful princess who must see past the ugly exterior and heal the man with her inner (and outer) beauty. There are no tales of handsome princes kissing female frogs! Even the ugly duckling, who eventually overcomes hardship and a lack of acceptance by evolving into a swan, is male.

A fairy-tale princess often doesn't have to do very much at all to win the hand of her prince, either, does she? She is often merely decorative. Sleeping Beauty was able to seduce while in a coma. Snow White attracted the prince while she was in a glass coffin. (Is it just me, or is the fact he desired a seemingly dead woman creepy?) Cinderella managed to secure a marriage proposal after just one date. I used to sometimes torment myself when I was young, trying to think of what she did on that date that was so amazing so I could replicate it. Had she told brilliant jokes? Did she do a particularly captivating version of the Chicken Dance at the ball? And how did she pull off funny and groovy, all while wearing glass slippers? I suspected I would have spent the whole night whingeing and plastering my heels in Band-Aids.

These stories shape our childhood notions of femininity and relationships — and they don't stop having an impact on us, do they? The princess myth follows us into our teen years, and adult years as well. Just think about how many films aimed at teens are princess focused.

> **femininity**: a socially and culturally accepted version of what it means to be female that is learnt, often through popular culture

My big fat princess wedding

Think, too, about how many young women want the princess fantasy to be enacted on their real-life princess day — their wedding day. Brides-to-be often say it will be the one day when they get to dress and act like a princess. Some women choose to arrive at the ceremony in a horse-drawn carriage, and traditional wedding dresses look fit for a princess. And, thanks to TV reality shows that allow us an insight into the minds of brides-to-be, it's apparent that many women feel extraordinary pressure to get everything just right on this one big dream day.

I find it unsettling that more thought may go into details such as selecting the right flowers and menu for the day than into what the couple's relationship will be like after this event. For some women, there seems to be an assumption that getting the wedding day right is all that matters, and that the perfect wedding will, as if by magic, bring eternal happiness.

For many, the trappings of love — the size of the diamond in the engagement ring, the size of the bill for the wedding day — seem to be viewed as a measure of one's love. Planning for a wedding is something of a giant shopping trip for some people. 'Throughout, the bride is encouraged from all sides — by wedding magazines, by the coverage of celebrity weddings, and by the vendors she encounters — to think of herself as a "princess for a day",' according to Rebecca Mead, who wrote a book about the wedding industry. It's no wonder that people are spending big on weddings, 'given that a princess is one who enjoys limitless wealth and childish irresponsibility'.[2]

Fairy tales are also stories about social mobility, aren't they? Girls are elevated from working class to royalty. Cinderella's is a literal rags-to-riches tale. And if, in real life, a girl's husband-to-be is not actually wealthy, the couple can at least put on a show of wealth. Cue white doves! Cue violins! Cue rose petals!

When I was a young woman, I got particularly caught up in the notion that a girl's future partner would elevate her social standing. In many of the teen romance books I read, once the girl was noticed by the cool boy, she gained instant playground cred. You know the stereotype, right? The brainiac loses the glasses and undoes her ponytail — as if that's all it takes to move from 'Plain Jane' to uber-hottie — and lands the jock. Everyone, not just him, now loves her! She gets invited to all the best parties! The end!

Reclaiming the word 'princess'

When I work in schools with young women, because I've just met them I don't know everyone's name, so I tend to use terms of endearment such as 'sweetheart', 'gorgeous' and, yes, I did once use 'princess'. A teen girl at a school in Sydney turned around and glared at me. 'I am not a princess,' she said. 'I'm a vampire.' What an original response!

I asked her why my use of the term 'princess' had upset her. She explained that often the term is used as an insult to imply another girl is spoilt or a bit precious, as in, 'Suck it up, princess!' or 'Stop being such a princess!'

I agreed that she was absolutely correct, and went on to explain that I like to reclaim the word. After all, a princess isn't necessarily a girl with 'limitless wealth and childish irresponsibility' at all. A princess is, technically, a young girl or woman who may one day rule the kingdom. A young girl or woman who potentially has great power.

In fact, my all-time favourite fictional character is a kick-butt princess: super-heroine Wonder Woman, who is really the alter ego of Princess Diana of the Amazons, a nation of women warriors in Greek mythology. Not only does WW rock some amazing star-spangled knickers, but she fights crime using possibly one of the coolest super-tools ever, the Golden Lasso of Truth, which compels baddies to speak honestly to her. In the early days of the comics, though, the lasso's power was broader than that: if Wonder Woman caught you in her lasso, you had to obey all her commands.

The writer who created Wonder Woman back in the 1940s, William Marston, said the lasso was a symbol of 'female charm, allure, oomph, attraction' and the power that 'every woman has … over people of both sexes whom she wishes to influence or control in any way'.[3] Marston proved that you don't have to be a woman to be a feminist: when it came to creating a weapon to put in his super-heroine's hand, he didn't just adapt one of the many traditional masculine examples he could have chosen from. Instead, he recognised the power of femininity and turned it into a weapon itself. Wonder Woman doesn't just sit around waiting for a prince to come and bestow love on her. She grabs love in both her hands and uses it as a tool to restore peace and justice to the world.

Another fabulous antidote to the princess myth is *The Paper Bag Princess*, a children's story that I tell in my workshops.[4] In this picture book, Princess Elizabeth and her beloved Prince Ronald find their castle under siege by a dragon who steals Ronald away. As the castle has been destroyed, all Elizabeth can find to wear to go and rescue him is a paper bag. Throughout her quest, she outsmarts the dragon on numerous occasions and eventually marches in, triumphant, to rescue her man. Ronald looks at her with her paper-bag dress and messy tangled hair and tells her, 'Come back when you are dressed like a real princess.' (I love that when I am reading the story to teen girls, at this point someone will usually yell out, 'Oh no, he didn't!')

Feisty, brave Elizabeth tells Ronald that while he looks like a real prince, he is in fact a toad. And, we are told, 'they didn't get married after all'. The final image shows a jubilant, free-looking Princess Elizabeth skipping off into the sunset — solo. Bam!

And you know what? Despite all the fairy tales we read that groomed us for marriage, I suspect that when we were little girls we instinctively knew that the message that we should pair up no matter what was nonsense.

Same goes for all the pretty-pink toy marketing hype. Sure, we may have embraced princess and fairy props such as crowns, wands and sparkly dresses, but we didn't pop them on, then wait poised for a prince to come and rescue us! I believe girls use princess- and fairy-themed props to play at power. They order around servants. Right wrongs within their kingdom. Grant wishes. True?

When my daughter, Teyah, was four years old, she was a complete Snow White devotee. Yet there was no cleaning up after dwarfs or lying in glass coffins for her, thank you very much! She was known as the Gumboot

Princess by her preschool mates, because under her princess gown she always wore sensible boots — all the better for stomping around to create order.

The reality is that many children play in creative and even subversive ways. You may well have quite literally deconstructed Barbie by pulling her arms off or chopping at her hair. Or, as I did as a little girl, perhaps you ignored the pretty-pink Barbie Kitchen and instead drove Barbie around in a makeshift car, pretending she was building an empire.

> subversive: acting to overturn accepted ways of thinking or doing things

I love that as little girls we were, at times, able to instinctively pull apart limiting messages and reinvent popular culture to suit ourselves. Let's reclaim that power.

By thinking critically about movies, TV shows, books and ads, and by developing the skills you need to understand the messages they send, you will be a truly powerful princess — with or without a tiara and prince.

Say no to the crazy cat lady myth

The often shocking way single women were treated historically may help explain why we sometimes feel so vulnerable and unsettled when we don't have a partner.

In the sixteenth and seventeenth centuries, a particular type of religious zeal, driven largely by men, took hold in Europe and led to tens of thousands of people being branded as witches. Approximately 100,000 supposed witches were put to death, and most of them were women. Those accused of witchcraft were often poor, older single women who lacked male protection.[5]

And here we see, perhaps, the real origins of the lonely cat lady myth. Cats were viewed as a witch's 'familiar' — that is, a spirit friend living in the body of her pet. Often, a single woman's ownership of a cat was considered evidence enough to execute not just her, but her pet as well. In fact, cat burning became a morbid type of entertainment in France during the 1700s.

In the eighteenth century in England, women felt they had very little choice but to marry. They were not given the same educational opportunities as boys and were banned from universities; therefore, the jobs available to them paid low wages. The only path to financial security was through marriage; laws were based on the assumption that a woman's husband would take financial care of her.

Women also couldn't own land, and all inheritance was passed down from father to son. This made women vulnerable, because without a financially stable marriage they would be left destitute. To prevent their daughters from meeting this unfortunate fate, wealthy aristocratic parents would offer a large sum of money, known as a dowry, to the family of an eligible groom in exchange for their daughter's protection. (By the way, this is where today's tradition of the bride's family paying for the wedding comes from.) If a poor woman was able to secure the love of a wealthy man, she may be able to advance her family's fortune by 'marrying up', but without a dowry, his family would very likely refuse to allow the wedding to go ahead. So marriage was not the romantic union we view it as today. It was a serious financial transaction that allowed wealthy families to align themselves with other wealthy families, while love and romance took a back seat. For many women, the duty to marry well produced great sadness. Once she was stuck in a loveless marriage, a woman often became isolated from her family and friends, her risk of domestic violence increased, and she had no option but to fulfil her conjugal duties in the bedroom.

> conjugal: relating to the sexual relationship between a husband and wife

Of course there were women who bucked the trend. Susan B. Anthony was a nineteenth-century American educator and activist who worked towards gaining women the right to vote. Her rationale? 'I declare to you that woman must not depend upon the protection of man, but must be taught to protect herself, and there I take my stand.'

Bucking the trend was a big risk, though. During Victorian times, women could be accused of being insane if they made too much of a fuss about their lot. In fact, if a woman expressed something that the male doctors of the day did not agree with, they could deem her words as hysterical ramblings. The term 'hysterical' derives from the Greek word meaning 'womb' (hence the term 'hysterectomy' for the type of surgery in which a woman's uterus is removed). Historically, society would have us believe some deep flaw within our wombs could literally make us insane!

Women could also be sent to mental asylums for having an affair or being considered too sexually excitable. Single women were particularly at risk of being accused of these misdeeds.

And thus we see the beginnings of the stigmatisation of single women as crazy.

> stigmatisation: the showing of strong disapproval for a person or group of people

There are still plenty of double standards today when we discuss single women compared to single men. Think about it. The terms we use to describe a single man make it sound as though he is having a ball *doing* the coolest things and having many a wild romance. He is a player, playboy, ladies' man, lady-killer, womaniser, pick-up artist, bachelor, stud.

At best, a single woman might be referred to as a bachelorette, which implies that all she is doing is *waiting* for her husband to come along. If she isn't waiting passively for a man to find her — or desperately in pursuit of a man — she can expect a huge backlash. Single women who dare to get close to guys without officially becoming someone's girlfriend are at risk of being called a slut, a skank or a whore. Note that I said 'get close to' — girls don't even have to do anything sexual to risk being called these terms, do they?

'When I started being [considered] a slut I was fourteen years old and still a virgin,' writes Emily Maguire in her fantastic book for girls, *Your Skirt's Too Short*. She goes on to say that at her school, as at most schools, a girl could be considered a slut simply for wearing eyeliner or rolling down the waistband of her skirt: 'Slut-status did not depend on having sex but on people thinking that you did.'[6]

Although as single girls today we are able to own property and are not at risk of being burnt alive with our pets, there is still a lot of work to do before society truly feels comfortable with girls who are flying solo.

We still burn girls who are seen as pushing boundaries — now we just choose to burn them with our words.

Having a me party!

So, if we are reclaiming not just our princess power but also our worth as single girls (with or without kittens), what might the single time in our lives be like?

> It's all about you. You don't have to be committed to anything all the time. It gives you time and space to focus on you and making yourself happy. In my opinion, making sure you are as happy as possible is far more important than being in a relationship, and

if you are truly happy, then you have the ability to make your partner happy. :)

Brinley, 15

Vanessa decided she would deliberately remain single 'in every sense of the word. No men, no dating, no flirting, no kisses, no romantic love, no Valentine's Day, nothing' for 1000 days in order to find out just what her life might be like without the distraction of romance. She wrote:

This is a choice. Until March 14, 2015, I am choosing to be alone. And what I choose to do with that time, I think, will define me later on. I intend to use this time to address some of the issues I have ...

I also feel ... that life at times seems to revolve around love-dating-men-women-sex-flirting-breakups-makeups-lovesongs-romantic comedies ...

Is there a life outside of it all?

Well, I intend to find out ...

In choosing to remain single for the next 1000 days, I won't necessarily lack love in my life. In fact, it is quite the contrary. I have begun discovering just how much love I have in my life. It's always been there, and I've always felt I was well loved, but without the distraction of trying to stay afloat in a tumultuous relationship, I am beginning to see the extent of it ...[7]

Sounds exciting, huh?

It can seem so very urgent that we find a partner, especially when we're young. But later on, when we look back on our lives, we might have a different perspective, as does my friend, author and journalist Susan Johnson:

> There's a huge difference in being alone, and being lonely. I can safely say that I am rarely ever lonely — I have such a full, rich life, made up of my dearest women friends, my dear male friends, my family, my colleagues — that it is a great fat private joy for me to spend an hour, or a day, or a week alone. I relish the quiet of it, the chance to reflect, the chance to dance in my underpants with the music up loud and not have to worry if I look like a dork.
>
> It took me years to understand that I am not defined by whether or not I have a husband or a boyfriend. These days I would only consider letting a man fully enter my life if he added something to it, something wonderful — I just don't want him in my life simply because he is a man. He has to be the right man — kind, interesting, funny. Not perfect (because I'm not perfect) but just right for me.
>
> I've had boyfriends and husbands for most of my life but ever since I turned fifty I've realised that it's not really necessary to have a man in order to have a rich, fulfilling life. A man is a bonus, a little added extra, but — finally, at long last — I know now in my deepest self that a man does not need to

> *be the central plank of one's existence. I love men, but I no longer need them in the way I did when I was younger. Wish I knew then what I know now!*

Eighteen-year-old Jemma also has a refreshing perspective:

> *Being single for me wasn't just a waiting zone. I wasn't just hanging out in single town waiting for someone to ask me out so I could pass go and collect 200 dollars! Single can be a choice. Yes, we all want to love and be loved, but that doesn't mean that every single person is desperate and dateless and up late worrying about a life with 900 cats! I chose single. Well, actually, I chose school, which meant I chose single for a while. But there's no shame in that. The way I see it, I chose me. I had a lovely boy, who I knew would be a super boyfriend, and boy did I like him. I just loved me more.*

There are many wonderful things about being single in addition to being able to dance in your undies without worrying about looking like a dork — which is a solid enough reason on its own, in my humble opinion. Here are a few more to contemplate:

- You can spend more time with your friends.
- You can watch the movies you like without having to negotiate.

- You can focus on your schoolwork, part-time job, art project or singing career. (Hey, you sound like you've got it going on!)
- You don't have to make small talk with his friends and family. This can be challenging if you don't really relate to them, can't it?
- You can learn more about you rather than focus all your energy on learning about him.

I love teen girl Ella's optimistic take on being single: 'Boys might just be too intimidated by your magnificence to approach you. Also: you're not forever alone, you're forever available.' Amen, sista!

Single can suck sometimes

Despite all this 'single and loving it!' talk, I recognise that there are some times in a single girl's life that prove particularly challenging — even to the most self-assured of us. It's OK to admit this. You don't need to be Wonder Woman all the time. Let me help you learn how to deal with these.

Single can suck when ...

1. You have no date for the formal.

For many girls, the practice event for being a bride/princess is the school formal.

I asked the teen girls who are fans of Enlighten Education's Facebook page to share their thoughts on having a date for the school formal. They were so incredibly perceptive and honest. (Enlighten's fans are the best. Fact.)

> Finding a date that you think everyone will like and won't judge you for is actually the worst form of stress! It is just as bad as finding an outfit, and that's tough.

Victoria, 17

> It's a lot of pressure thinking that everyone else will have a date and you're going to be by yourself, and you get self-conscious thoughts, asking yourself why nobody has asked you and whether people will laugh at you.

Lisa, 16

> I'm nineteen and still haven't had a boyfriend, possibly in part due to going to a private girls' school without much opportunity to make friends who were guys. I went to my Year 11 formal with a bunch of my friends who also didn't have boyfriends and had a fantastic time, but I did not go to my Year 12 formal at all because I didn't want to go alone. I don't regret not going, but I might someday. The pressure is mostly my own upon myself, with some indirect pressure from others gushing about buying matching ties and corsages. I dealt with it by being a bit of a chicken and avoiding it altogether!

Jessie, 19

I think that the biggest pressure is finding a date for your formal, mostly because I go to an all-girls school. It is definitely a lot of pressure for a teenager. I think most of the pressure [comes from] parents as they think everyone will have a date but you. Most girls say it is fine to not take a date. :)

Jamie, 17

It's hard because there is so much stereotyping nowadays. Sometimes I feel like I have to go with someone who is older than me or the same age ... And if you go with a guy who is just a friend, everyone thinks you are in love with each other ... But we all just have to try and ignore the rumours and move on ... As cliché as that sounds, and as hard as it really is, it's so, so true!!!

Elizabeth, 17

See? You are not alone. Sometimes I think just knowing you are not the only one to experience doubt and apprehension helps. Agree?

The following tips for surviving formal time as a single girl will also help:

- As a solo operator, you will be able to really enjoy the company of your schoolmates and celebrate all your in-jokes together (which is, after all, what an end-of-school formal is supposed to be about).

- Think about all the girls who will look back at pictures from the night and cringe when they see who they went with just because they felt pressured to pair up. Trust me, I was this girl!
- If you are dateless, you will be free to meet, dance or flirt with other singles.
- Take a whole group of single besties (boys and girls) and be one another's dates. Rock up in a stretch limo and release white doves. Own it!

2. You don't have a Valentine on Valentine's Day.
I had been single for six months when I was writing this chapter. Most of the time, I felt genuinely excited about what the future might look like, and I knew it would be grand, with or without a partner. However, there were some things that sent me falling into a spiral of self-despair, such as when I saw a card in a newsagency that read 'Happy birthday to my darling wife'. What if no-one ever bought me a card like that again? I had received my share of romantic cards in the past, from my ex-husband and ex-boyfriend, but I wanted more! Was I doomed to a card-less life? Curse you, Hallmark! *Danni waves her fist in the air.*

Well, take that pain and multiply it to the power of ten and you get Valentine's Day for singles. True? Suddenly the world is filled with playful cards for cool couples to giggle at together, and mushy cards for the old-school romantic types. Oh, it's a day for lovers.

And don't they love sharing their love (read: flaunting it)? When I used to teach in high schools, it always amused me that many girls relished carrying around their cards, flowers and teddy bears all day. They didn't leave them in their lockers — oh no, half the thrill was in showing them off. And it seemed that the bigger the bear, the bigger the love must be.

I really don't begrudge those who are struck by Cupid. Love is a beautiful thing worth acknowledging — every day, not just on Valentine's Day. I really am a romantic at heart, too.

But when you're on the outside of it all, it can sting.

I called Nina after the 'no cards for me' incident and she gave me such great advice: receiving a card like that never makes someone feel as wonderful as it makes those who don't receive one feel worthless. 'It's a whole big mind mess-up,' she said. 'Don't fall for the Hallmark moments.'

See why I love Nina? See? Gold star for relationship advice!

And you know what? One of the best Valentine's Days I ever had was when I was single. I decided to tackle the day head-on. I invited all my single friends over for dinner and encouraged them to bring each of the other guests a card, chocolate or flower. We ate, laughed and were merry.

And in addition to the very funny and thoughtful gifts I received from my guests that night, I actually did receive amazing bouquets of flowers from two guys who liked me but understood all I could offer them was friendship. They just weren't quite right for me, and I wasn't going to compromise.

In my experience, the more you have going on in your life and the more comfortable you are being single, the more other people will want to be with you. You will also be less likely to just jump into any old relationship so you can have the 'Hallmark moment'.

Apart from throwing a 'Single and Fab!' party like I did (or as one friend likes to call it, a 'Galentine' party to celebrate your best gals), you might like to try the following ideas for coping with Valentine's Day when you're single:

- Focus on all the love you have in your life. Give handwritten notes (or cards and flowers if that's your thing) to your best friends and favourite family members. I always feel better when I am loving towards others; some of the love definitely bounces back.
- Be daring. Send a note or a card to someone you have a crush on. (Do it anonymously if you prefer; Valentine's cards were traditionally meant to be sent by secret admirers.) It will be quite thrilling — trust me. A friend of mine and I did it when we were in the senior years of high school, and writing out our notes, hunting down our

crushes' addresses and then mailing them off was such delicious, laugh-until-you-snort fun!
- Author Emily Maguire offered me this top-shelf suggestion: 'Young single women who love all the hoopla associated with Valentine's Day ... could consider embracing it all for a good cause. Like organise a red-velvet-swathed, heart-shaped, chocolate-filled, white-teddy-bear-decorated, romcom-screening fundraising event for a related cause such as marriage equality or safe-sex education.'
- Go totally Grinch and have an anti-Valentine's Day party. I'm talking about getting together with your friends and watching horror movies rather than romantic comedies, wearing your PJs rather than party frocks and making the talk a relationships-free zone!
- Take some time out to do a loving kindness meditation. It's an ancient Buddhist practice in which you sit quietly and wish love, peace and happiness on the people in your life, including yourself and even people you dislike. People who do it regularly boost the feel-good chemicals in their brains and make themselves more likely to experience loving moments in everyday life — basically,

they become their own love factories. After studying this effect, the psychologist Barbara Fredrickson believes it's time to rethink our whole concept of what love is. The passionate, romantic, *Romeo and Juliet* type of love may be more of a myth, while true love is all the little moments when you have a positive emotional connection with another person during your day. Sure, you might have such a moment with a romantic partner, but you just as easily might have one with a good friend, your little sister or that random person who just held the door open for you because you had your hands full. 'If you don't have a Valentine, that doesn't mean that you don't have love,' says Fredrickson.[8]

3. Your friends and family won't stop asking why you don't have a boyfriend yet.

It can be unsettling when everyone seems to think your relationship status is their business, can't it?

Try calling them out on the impact their words are having on you. They may be completely unaware they are upsetting you. You don't need to be confrontational, just honest: 'I find you asking me about this makes me feel pressured. It also makes me feel as if my life as a single girl isn't interesting to you. How about if you agree to let the topic go, and I'll promise that you'll be among the first to know when, and if, I get a new partner — fair enough?'

If you have a friend who makes you feel uncomfortable by continually asking why you're single, is it possible they are really a frenemy? You can't pick your family, but you can pick your friends. If the relationship you have with a buddy is becoming toxic and making you feel less, demand more! It is important to surround yourself with positive people, because outside of your family, your friendship group may be your main source of affection and attention. Perhaps focus on finding your BFFs first, and worry later about finding love.

You can always baffle them with numbers: one in ten Australians live alone, mostly women. And these singles are not necessarily lonely. Countries with high levels of people living alone actually score well on happiness ratings.[9] You could finish off by saying something like 'Seeing I am still young, I don't think we need panic yet. But even if I stay single forever, it seems I will be just dandy!'

And remember, if you do find someone who makes your heart sing, be mindful of your friends who have not yet.

Find, love and enjoy you. And support your single mates to do likewise.

Whether you find someone to love or not, you'll be fabulous either way. Because you, gorgeous girl, are already whole.

Quiz

Circle the answer that comes closest to describing your situation.

1. When you are single, you search those cute-couple Tumblr pages:

   A. Daily. And then you go and cry because you're not basking in sunlight, looking into someone's gorgeous eyes.
   B. Occasionally. It can be fun (and sometimes funny) to check out romance land.
   C. Never. Romance sucks.

2. If you are single and are asked to join your best friend and her new partner at the movies, you:

   A. Go, but only if she promises that they'll bring someone you can get with, too.
   B. Ask her if you could bring along a mutual friend so it doesn't feel quite so awkward for you being the 'third wheel'.
   C. Don't go. How dare she ask you — does she actually like humiliating you?

3. If you are single and see that a close friend's status on Facebook has changed to 'In a Relationship', you:

   A. Immediately hassle her to see if her new partner has any friends you might like.
   B. Let her know how happy you are for her.

C. Feel gutted. And angry with yourself for being such a failure.

4. When a guy you are not sure you really like asks you to be his girlfriend, you:

A. Accept. Beggars can't be choosers.
B. Tell him no, respectfully (see Nina's tips on how to end a relationship in the Q&A section). You're not going to have a boyfriend just for the sake of it.
C. Tell him off. How dare he think *you'd* like *him*?

5. When you go to a party without a date, the first thing you do is:

A. Check out whether there are any cute singles.
B. Give everyone you greet a big 'howdy'.
C. Sit in the corner sulking all night and feeling tragic about being alone while it seems as if everyone around you is hooking up.

6. You're single and see a really beautiful friendship ring at the jeweller's. You:

A. Have a meltdown because there is no-one to buy it for you.
B. Buy it for yourself! Hey, you're worth spoiling.
C. Decide it's tacky and pathetic. Girls who flaunt stuff their boyfriends give them are just lame.

7. There is a girl at your school who is rumoured to have got into a heavy kissing session with a guy she isn't dating. When a friend of yours refers to the girl as a 'skank', you:

   A. Join in the slut-shaming session. And feel secretly jealous that she got a kiss when you didn't.
   B. Remind your friend that there were two people kissing; if your friend thinks it was acceptable for the guy to be kissing, it should be acceptable for the girl, too. Besides, it's never OK to label guys or girls in a negative way.
   C. Join in the slut-shaming session. And spread the story throughout your year group.

Now add up how many A's, B's and C's you circled, and check below.

Mostly A's

You have fallen into the trap of believing that the state of being single is a condition that needs to be cured. Try to focus on all the things that are fantastic about being solo and use some of the 'Single can suck when ...' tips to help you through challenging times.

Mostly B's

You have a strong sense of self and are rockin' life. Your positivity means you will always be surrounded by love, whether it comes from a romantic partner, your inner circle of buddies or your family.

Mostly C's

You seem to be letting your desire to find a partner cloud your sense of what is already working in your life. When we focus only on the negatives, we risk becoming bitter and start to see the world through dark-coloured glasses. You need to spend some more time focusing on what is great about this stage in your life and develop some strategies to help you when you feel left out or lonely.

Affirmations

I am worthy of love.

I surround myself with positive people and bring good things into my life.

I am complete.

So true!! x

CHAPTER 9

Relationship Q&A

by Nina

Crushes and dating

Q. My parents think I'm too young to start dating. How young is too young?

A. Knowing the right time to start dating isn't so much about waiting till you turn a specific age. It's about 'taking the time to do it right', according to psychologist Jacqui Manning. 'Your early relationships can really set the scene for your love future, so having good experiences now will set you up with positive expectations from your partners forever.'

Ask your parents why they think you're too young. Ask for their advice, and ask whether they're comfortable to share their own experiences with you. Although some girls find it uncomfortable to talk about relationships with their parents, you can get some good tips by having an honest chat with them.

Relationships can be difficult to manage when you're still busy learning about yourself, so don't rush into it just because it's what other people are doing, says Jacqui. 'The important thing to remember is to not get swept up in another person's idea of how the relationship should be, but to establish your own values and boundaries around what's important to you — *before* you enter into a relationship. That way, you'll have a better idea of when something doesn't feel right.'

Before dating, think about the following questions: what kind of person do I like and what sort of qualities am I looking for in a person? What are my dating boundaries and deal breakers? What would a good relationship look and feel like to me? If, after you have put some effort into thinking about what you want, you feel self-assured enough to set boundaries in your relationships, then you may well be ready to get out there.

Q. I'm sixteen and I have a crush on a guy at work who's nineteen. I'm pretty sure he likes me back, because he's always flirting with me. What should I do about it?

A. There are a few things you need to consider before getting into a relationship with anyone at work: does your workplace have a specific policy about co-workers dating? What would happen if you broke up? Would one of you need to leave your job? If so, who would that be? Is one of you in a higher role, or responsible for supervising the other person at work? That can create all sorts of problems in a relationship, and your co-workers may feel that there is 'special treatment' going on. Also, is your flirting at work making your co-workers feel uncomfortable?

Then you also need to consider the issue of dating someone older than you. While girls generally mature quicker than boys and three years may not seem like a huge age gap, there is still a big difference between most sixteen-year-olds and nineteen-year-olds. For starters, nineteen-year-olds might be going to university or TAFE or beginning a more serious career, while most sixteen-year-olds are still in school. Nineteen-year-olds are able to enter places that you are not, such as bars, clubs and pubs. You need to work out whether you have enough in common to make a relationship work.

Q. I have a physical disability and I often feel that other people overlook me when it comes to love and dating. Do you have any advice?
A. This is such an important question that I brought in my friend Stella Young, a disability activist, comedian and editor, to answer it:

When I was younger, I vowed that I would never have a relationship with another disabled person. Certainly until I was about seventeen, I was kind of 'in the closet' about disability. I knew I had one — heck, I got my first motorised wheelchair when I was two and a half — but I did my very best not to acknowledge it. I didn't hang out with other disabled people (ew!) and I would certainly have never entertained the prospect of a relationship with one.

In fact, teenage-me thought that if I could snag myself a non-disabled boyfriend, that meant I'd made it. I'd win the battle to just be 'a normal person' like everyone else. I'd blend seamlessly into the crowd and wheel off into the sunset with my perfectly proportioned prince.

Then, something happened. I read a book about the 'social model' of disability. The social model says that disability isn't actually about what's 'wrong' with our bodies or our brains, it's about the things that make it hard for us to get along in the world. So my disability is caused by the fact that there aren't always enough ramps and disabled toilets for me to get around in my wheelchair. It gave me a whole new way of thinking about myself. I realised that a huge part of my reluctance to have a relationship with someone else with a disability stemmed from the fact that I was still viewing disability as my own personal deficiency. Once I realised that many of the issues in my life stem from society and the environment, everything changed. Realising that disabled people are not wrong for the world we live in, but that the world is simply not yet right for us, was enormously liberating.

It is often assumed that sexuality is a concept that simply doesn't apply to people with disabilities. I wasn't asked by a doctor if I was sexually active until I was twenty-seven. I always had to volunteer that information. Some doctors even responded with blatant surprise. This isn't exactly encouraging from some of the most highly educated members of our communities, is it?

Because of all this discomfort around sexuality and disability, it's no wonder that having a relationship at all can feel like an act of rebellion. In many ways, it seems the path of least resistance is for us to have a relationship with someone else with a disability. Society seems to be more comfortable if we 'stick with our own kind'. This attitude used to apply to interracial relationships as well, and some people are still quite uncomfortable with that!

If I could go back and talk to my teenage self, this is what I'd tell her:

- Be proud of who you are.
- Don't look for someone who's going to like you because they 'look past' your disability. Your disability is part of you, and not something anyone should ignore.
- Other people with disabilities are actually pretty cool to hang out with, and to date. Being with someone who experiences the world a bit like you do is absolutely wonderful.

- *There will be some people you like who won't like you back, but it won't always be about disability.*

So you're in a relationship ... now what?

Q. How do I know if my partner is the one?

A. First things first. On a planet of 7 billion people there isn't only one person out there whom you will be able to build a stable, loving relationship with. This is great news when you think about it, because the odds of finding a single needle in a 7-billion-strong haystack are minuscule. The second thing is that different people are right for us at different points in life. During your teens and twenties, you are still growing and changing a lot, so it's not uncommon to find that whom you are compatible with may change.

How can you tell if someone is compatible with you? (Hint: it takes a little more than having compatible star signs!) Start by reviewing your relationship values list that you made in Chapter 1. Does your partner share similar relationship values? Or do you find that you differ in some core ways? When it comes to your relationship, do you feel you are on the same page? And how does the relationship make you feel on an average day? Some signs of a good relationship include:

- You respect and listen to each other, and value each other's opinions.

- You can be yourself around your partner, and vice versa.
- You feel safe and supported, and the relationship makes you both deeply happy.
- You trust each other.
- You're not just partners, you're also friends.
- You support each other's goals in life.
- You respect each other's rights to your own feelings, values, friends, activities and beliefs.
- You are both honest and accountable for your own actions, and you can both admit when you're wrong.
- You can communicate openly and truthfully with each other.
- You share the decision-making. You try to make fair decisions. If you cannot mutually agree on something, you are both willing to compromise.
- You seek mutually satisfying resolutions to conflict. You each talk and act so that the other feels safe and comfortable to express himself or herself.

Q. My boyfriend works more than I do, so he spends more money on gifts for birthdays and Christmas. I don't want him to think I don't value him. What should I do?

A. People express their love and appreciation in different ways, which fall into five main categories:

1. **Words.** Compliments, kind words and thankyous build your partner's confidence and make them feel valued.
2. **Actions.** There are practical things you can do out of love to help your partner, lighten their load or make their day that much brighter. Errands, chores and small tasks might not sound very romantic, but when done out of kindness these things can really make someone feel cared for.
3. **Thoughtful gift giving.** Gifts don't have to be expensive to show that you love the person. What makes a gift special is the level of thought that goes into it.
4. **Quality time.** Spending time together and focusing on each other is a great way to show affection, so if you have been spending a lot of time hanging out with groups of friends, try giving each other some undivided attention.
5. **Touch.** Showing someone you care through touch is not necessarily sexual. Holding hands, rubbing someone's back or giving them a neck massage are all ways of showing you care.[1]

While all five ways of showing love are important, they matter to different people in different amounts. Having a clear idea of what matters most to your partner (and vice versa), and understanding that you may have different ways of expressing your affection is important. An ex-boyfriend of mine was terrible at gift giving: he once gave me plastic flowers because he thought they were better value than the real thing as they last longer. Deep down he had a heart of gold. While he was terrible at choosing gifts, he showed he cared in all sorts of other ways, such as making nice dinners and giving back massages.

To determine your own preference, ask yourself: how do I express love to others? And which of the five do I request the most often? Then think about how your partner would answer those same questions. Better yet, ask your partner.

Q. My parents don't want my boyfriend to stay the night, even though they know we are already in a sexual relationship. We love each other and really want to be able to stay at each other's places. What should we do? (We are both seventeen.)

A. Around the world, parents are strongly divided on the sleepover question. In some countries, like the Netherlands, it is fairly typical for parents to allow teenage couples to have sleepovers, and research there consistently shows that teens are less likely to have unsafe sex as a result.

However, many other parents feel uncomfortable with the idea of teens having sleepovers, especially if one or both teenagers are under the age of consent. In your case, you are both over the age of consent, but your parents may have other reasons for not allowing your boyfriend to stay the night.

In addition to religious or cultural beliefs, some parents don't allow teens' partners to sleep over because they believe that their children are not emotionally ready to handle everything that goes with a sexual relationship. Alternatively, some parents worry about the presence of younger siblings in the house who might be confused about the nature of the relationship. Your parents might be concerned about the amount of time you are spending with your boyfriend and the impact that is having on other areas of your life. The point is that you won't know what your parents' reasons are unless you talk to them about it.

When you raise the issue, be open to what your parents have to say. Put your point of view forward, but do so respectfully and hear them out. See if you can find a compromise. Finally, remember that your parents may change their minds over time, once they see you are in a stable relationship or once they get to know your partner a little better.

Q. My partner's parents disapprove of our relationship and make it pretty clear that they don't like me. What should I do?
A. It never feels good when other people reject you, particularly if those people happen to mean a lot to the person you are dating. Here are some steps to help

you cope when your partner's family is against your relationship:

1. **Don't take it personally.** It may feel personal, but unless you are being rude or disrespectful, you are not the one with the problem. You cannot control other people, so try to take a step back from the situation and put up some emotional boundaries.
2. **Don't drive a wedge.** Forcing your partner to choose between their family and you will not only stress your partner out, it is also likely to backfire — after all, your partner has known their family a lot longer than they have known you! Don't bad-mouth your partner's parents, and try to avoid putting your partner in the middle. Instead focus on the positives in your relationship.
3. **Try to understand where they are coming from.** There are many reasons why parents might oppose their child's choice of partner. Sometimes those reasons are legitimate — for instance, when their child's partner is controlling or self-destructive, or does things that are inappropriate or risky. At other times, parents do not know their child's partner well enough yet, or believe that their child and his/her partner don't have enough in common to sustain

a relationship. If this is the case, then understanding where they are coming from may help you deal with the situation.

However, sometimes parents oppose a relationship for more self-interested reasons. Parents who are fearful of losing control over their child's life will often view *any* relationship their child has as a threat — regardless of who the partner is.

And some parents oppose a relationship because they are unfairly prejudiced against certain groups of people based on their race, class, religion, appearance, sexual orientation and so on. If this is what you are dealing with, remember that their views are a reflection of them and them alone. Their opinions have nothing to do with you as an individual. It's not your responsibility to change other people's opinions, but you can rise above prejudice by being a role model of respect and tolerance yourself.

4. **Get to know them, they might change.** Sometimes we hit it off with people straight away, other times it takes a while. Give your partner's parents time to get to know you so that they have the chance to warm to you. A lot of parents eventually warm to their child's partner once they recognise

that their child is happy and that the relationship is meaningful.

5. **If they don't come around, stay true to yourself.** Not everyone is going to love you for the rock star that you are. We all crave acceptance and love, but the reality is that some people just never get along. If your partner's parents don't ever warm to you, then you can protect yourself from the sting of rejection by setting realistic expectations. For example, if you go to a family event, don't walk in thinking that they are going to be warm and enthusiastic to see you if your previous experience says otherwise. You'll only end up disappointed. Instead, say to yourself, 'My goal today is to be civil, respectful and maintain my boundaries in place.' By setting realistic expectations, you will stop getting as hurt or frustrated by the situation. Remind yourself of what it is that *you* value about yourself and the relationship. At the end of the day, you are dating your partner, not your partner's parents.

Friendship and dating

Q. I've got a crush on one of my best friends. Should I tell my friend or will this ruin the friendship?

A. Friendships can be an excellent basis for a relationship, because you already know and care about each other. But crushes can make things awkward between friends, especially if one is pining away for the other, who is just not that into them.

It's impossible to predict exactly what will happen if you tell your friend. Maybe your friend feels the same way about you — in which case, you two will probably become the most disgustingly adorable couple ever.

But maybe your friend doesn't. You won't know unless you ask, but if you do decide to talk to your friend about it, be prepared for the friendship to shift gears for a while. Your friend may need some space — and so may you — until things settle down again.

If you are ever in the reverse position and a friend confides that he or she has feelings for you, remember that it has taken tremendous guts and your friend is probably feeling very nervous and exposed. If you don't feel the same way about your friend, be gentle but firm so that your friend doesn't hold out hope. Again, you may both need a bit of space, but hopefully in time your friend will move on and things will settle and return to normal.

Q. My friend's boyfriend is cheating on her. How should I tell her?
A. Right now you're probably feeling a whole range of feelings, from anger and betrayal to frustration, worry and concern for your friend. But before you do anything, take a step back and answer these two questions:

1. Are you sure he is cheating? What evidence do you have? You don't want to rush off and tell your friend her boyfriend is cheating if you have unreliable info.
2. If you are sure he is cheating, who would she most want to hear the news from? Most people would prefer to hear it from their partner. If you believe this is the case, you might want to tell her boyfriend that you know and give him the opportunity to come clean to her. If he denies it or refuses to tell her, then you need to work out how to break the news.

The best way to tell a friend that her partner is cheating is face to face and in private. Be prepared for your friend to get upset and ask you a lot of questions. She will probably want to know who else knows about it, so don't gossip to other friends about the cheating. Even if you're simply trying to get their advice on how to break the news to your friend, she will only feel more humiliated if she thinks that she is the last to find out. Keep it to yourself and allow your friend to decide if she wants to tell people. Finally, be prepared to support your friend no matter what she decides to do with the information. She may break up with her boyfriend immediately. She might not. Either way, she's going to need a good friend by her side.

Q. I've recently developed feelings for my friend's boyfriend. I know that she plans to break up with him but is waiting until after our school formal so that she doesn't have to go alone. What should I do?

A. This is a pretty complicated situation because there are three people's feelings to consider: yours, hers and his. First up, let's address your friend's situation. Keeping a guy around just so that a girl has someone to spend her birthday/formal/Valentine's Day with is pretty deceptive (not in the least because the guy is often expected to shell out large amounts of money on the event). It's also quite horrible to have someone break up with you immediately after a special event.

But if you encourage her to break up with her boyfriend and she later finds out you liked him, chances are your friend will feel betrayed by you. She may think that you had a hidden motive for wanting her to break up with him before the formal — and let's be honest here, you kind of do. Telling him that your friend plans to break up with him is also not a good idea, as going behind her back may start a fight between you and her.

Perhaps it's time to come clean to your friend. If you choose to do that, begin by telling her how difficult it is for you to admit to her that you have feelings for her boyfriend. Give her space to come to terms with the situation. If she really is over him, she may be fine about breaking up with him. But there is also a chance that she may become jealous or angry. You cannot control her reaction, and it's still her decision whether or not to break up with him. Most of all, do your best not to involve other people. This is exactly the sort of thing that groups of people can end up taking sides on.

Finally, it is easy for love interests to come between good friends. Whether your friend breaks up with her boyfriend now or later, it's never a good idea to start anything with a friend's ex until some time has passed and everyone has had a chance to move on. When we're young, it's fairly normal for friends to date one another's exes, as the social circles we move in are limited and relationships are often short term. However, people's feelings can still easily get hurt, so it's important to give it some time. Then, when you think the timing is right, find out if your friend's ex reciprocates your feelings. If he does, and he wants to start something, then talk to your friend about the situation and be willing to hear her out. In the meantime, don't close down other options. After all, who knows who else you might meet!

Q. My friend just came out as a lesbian to my group of friends at school. This is new territory for all of us. How can we support her?

A. Because homophobic attitudes still exist, it often takes time for lesbian, gay and bisexual people to acknowledge their own sexual identity, both privately and publicly. If your friend is coming out to you, chances are that she has spent a good deal of time thinking about the situation and weighing up both the benefits and any potential risks of coming out.

Benefits to coming out often include feeling liberated, feeling as though you can talk more openly and honestly with your friends and family, being able to share important parts of your life with loved ones, feeling as though you don't have to censor yourself or hide things, and feeling acceptance from others for who you are. Some reasons why people may choose not to come out include the possibility of rejection, the belief that people will treat their sexual identity as 'just a phase', the risk of experiencing bullying, gossip or physical violence, the fear of being kicked out of home and the risk of discrimination.

The fact that your friend has chosen to tell you suggests that she must really trust you and believe that you will continue to accept and value her. To be supportive, here are some things you can do:

1. Remember that your friend is still the same person she was before she told you. More than anything, your friend probably wants to know that you guys are still cool and that you are not going anywhere. A positive, supportive response now will mean a great deal to her.
2. Don't ask, 'Are you sure?' or say that it is 'probably just a phase' or, worse, that she is 'just seeking attention'. It may have taken a lot of courage for your friend to tell you, so let her know you have heard her.

3. Don't ignore the situation. If you feel awkward about the news, glossing over it or laughing it off may make your friend feel as though you have not heard what she's told you. It's normal to have all different things race through your mind, but even if you feel awkward, you can still choose to validate her news by saying, 'Thank you for telling me.'
4. Figure out what your friend needs. For example, a friend who has come out to you because she is excited about a new relationship and wants you to be excited with her will likely want to celebrate. But a friend who has come out to you because she is upset that her parents are not supportive needs comfort and the knowledge that you are still there for her no matter what.
5. Realise that coming out is a process. People often come out in stages and choose to tell different people at different times. For example, just because someone has told her immediate friends and family, it doesn't mean she has told her extended family or distant friends. Respect your friend's right to decide if and when she lets other people know.
6. Find out more. There are loads of great websites and resources where you can find more information on this topic. We've listed some of our faves at the back of the book.

Never underestimate how powerful it is for your friend to have your support. A girl who attended one of Danni's workshops at school wrote her this email: 'After your program, I came out as bisexual to my friends and was loved and supported throughout that time. I am now a lot more confident in myself, and don't have as much trouble standing up for myself ... I want to thank you for helping me realise that there are people who can help, and that I'm never alone.'

Q. One of my friends always acts flirtatiously around my boyfriend. It makes me really uncomfortable but I don't know if I'm overreacting. What should I do about it?
A. Confronting a friend who is flirting with your boyfriend can be an awkward task but it's important that you talk to her. After all, if you don't address the situation, it is unlikely to change, right? But before you do, you might also want to ask your boyfriend how he feels about the situation. Maybe he hasn't noticed. Maybe he is flattered. But there is also a chance that he is feeling awkward about the situation and unsure of how to bring it up with you, so give him a chance to speak about it.

When you speak to your friend, be willing to give her some examples of her flirtatious behaviour, because some people are unaware that their actions are making others uncomfortable. If she is a good friend, she will respect your feelings. The following steps will help you prepare to talk to your friend — and you can use them any time you need to resolve a conflict with someone:

10 Steps to Conflict Resolution[2]

1. Plan ahead. Work out what you want to say so that you don't end up saying something you regret.
2. Seek advice. Find a mentor — such as a parent, older sister, cousin or someone else you trust — and get his or her advice on the situation and what you plan to say.
3. Offer time. Don't confront your friend when she is rushing off to catch a bus, do a test or is otherwise busy. Instead, tell your friend that there is something you want to talk to her about and ask her when a good time to talk would be.
4. Speak about it in person. Conflict resolution is best done face to face. Online you cannot see a person's body language or facial cues, and it's easy to misinterpret text messages and emails, because a person's tone is not always obvious. (Besides, having a discussion face to face will mean there is no written record of it that might get circulated later on!)
5. Keep it private. When you do meet up to talk, don't involve other people. Having an audience will only cause the situation to escalate.
6. Use 'I' statements instead of 'you' accusations. For example, instead of saying,

'Why do you always have to flirt with my boyfriend?', try saying, 'I feel that the way you act with my boyfriend is flirty and I feel hurt by this.' Accusations tend to make people defensive, so try to focus on how you are feeling and remember that you're here to address the problem, not attack the person.

7. Keep focus. Stick to the issue at hand and deal with one issue at a time. Don't bring up things that happened weeks or months ago that are not relevant to the issue you are discussing (like that time she borrowed and lost your favourite cardigan in Year 8). When you feel you're losing an argument or aren't being heard, it can be tempting to bring up other ammunition you have lying around. But this will only confuse the issue and distract you from your goal. If your friend tries to derail the conversation by bringing up other problems she has with you, acknowledge her concerns and agree to talk about those issues later, but tell her that those issues are separate and that you don't want to confuse the subject.

8. Expect to be heard. If your friend is texting or answering her phone while you are trying to talk to her, this is not respectful.

Ask if there is another time that you can speak to her when she won't be so distracted. You deserve to be heard.
9. Listen to your friend and give her time to respond. Both people need to express their feelings and points of view to create mutual understanding. She may have a totally different interpretation of the situation.
10. Seek agreement. The objective is not to defeat your opponent but to agree to a resolution or compromise. In this instance, if she apologises for her actions, acknowledge her apology and seek a commitment that she will change her flirty ways. If she doesn't acknowledge that she has done anything wrong, remain calm but assertive and listen to her reasoning. You don't have to agree with her, but give her the chance to speak. If it's impossible to resolve the situation, then it's OK for a friendship to be put on ice for a while. Despite what you might have been told in primary school, you don't actually have to be friends with everyone in life, and some friendships do end (or break down for a while). This doesn't mean that you should automatically start seeing her as an enemy, though. You can be friendly without having to be a friend.

Q. I don't like my friend's boyfriend. Do I tell her?
A. It's impossible to get along with everyone in life. But just because you don't like your friend's boyfriend, it doesn't mean you should automatically rush to tell her. Start by thinking about the following questions:

1. Why don't you like him?
2. Does he treat her respectfully?
3. Does he make her happy?

If you dislike your friend's boyfriend because you think he has bad hair, bad taste in music or an annoying laugh, that's something you might want to keep to yourself, especially if she hasn't even asked for your opinion. Everyone has different tastes.

If you're just feeling a bit left out because your friend doesn't spend all her free time with you any more, then the problem is not him personally. It's easy to feel left behind when a friend starts dating someone new, isn't it? But rather than taking it out on her boyfriend, you should talk to your friend about how you're feeling. Use lots of 'I' statements and suggest a solution: 'I really miss spending as much time with you. Perhaps we can make a time next week when just the two of us can catch up?' Chances are she is missing you, too, and together you can work at getting the friendship back on track.

However, if you don't like your friend's boyfriend because he doesn't respect her or doesn't seem to make her happy, that is a different story. She may or may not be open to talking about it. But you have every right to be concerned if your friend's partner puts her down, is jealous or possessive, makes her unhappy, or if she seems to have changed a lot since dating him — for instance, becoming more withdrawn or always agreeing with him.

You could try the following:

1. Ask her in a nonjudgmental tone what she enjoys about the relationship. Be open to hearing what she has to say. Later on, she'll be far more likely to come to you and be open about any relationship issues she's having if she doesn't feel that you are out to judge her.
2. Give voice to your concerns. Calmly explain what you have seen and how you feel. Avoid outright attacks on her boyfriend or comments that will shame her or make her defensive, such as 'How could you date such a jerk?' Be direct but sensitive and let her respond.
3. Remind her that you care about her, are on her side and will always be there for her. Knowing that she has supportive friends around her is important.

If your friend is in a relationship where there is physical, emotional or verbal abuse, this is very serious and you should speak to an adult about the situation. (For more information on unhealthy relationships and verbal, emotional and physical abuse, see Chapter 4.)

Be aware that if you raise the issue with your friend directly, she may become defensive or seek to protect her boyfriend. This is not uncommon, as controlling individuals are master manipulators and often condition their partners to be loyal at all costs. None of this is her fault. Try to keep the communication lines between you and her open.

It is also a good idea to speak to a trusted adult about your own feelings. Whether you feel worried, sad, helpless, frustrated, angry at him, angry at her, or any other emotion, these feelings are all totally normal, and talking about it will help you cope. Counselling hotlines are there to offer assistance to people who are in unhealthy relationships *and* their supporters, so if you want advice on the situation, or want to talk about how you are feeling about it, you can call.

Q. Is it ever OK to snoop through my partner's phone or Facebook messages? If they have nothing to hide, what is the problem?

A. Sharing Facebook and phone passwords may look like a sign of trust, but in fact, putting up healthy boundaries and respecting your partner's privacy is the ultimate sign of trust in a relationship. We all need some privacy. Even if your partner has nothing to hide and the two of you are honest and upfront with each other, it doesn't mean that you should be allowed to pry into each other's personal texts and emails. It's not healthy for someone to need or want to know every single detail of another person's life. Setting boundaries is a sign of a healthy, functioning relationship, not a sign that you and your partner don't trust each other!

In fact, even if you and your partner are fine about each looking through the other's texts and emails, it doesn't follow that the people who sent those texts and emails would be fine with it. This is especially so if those people believed they were sharing things with you or your partner in confidence. For instance, my good friend confidentially emailed me about problems she was having that she would have been embarrassed for other people to know about. If my boyfriend had gone through my emails (which he never would!), I know my friend would have been mortified (and probably a bit cranky with me, too).

There is a bigger issue here: why do you want to go snooping in the first place? It sounds as though you don't trust your partner. Snooping will only break down the trust further. You should talk to your partner about it. If your instincts tell you something is wrong or if your partner is acting unusually, then it is reasonable to ask them what is going on.

But if you find that you get easily jealous or if you need to keep tabs on where your partner is and what they are doing, then it sounds as though you have some difficulty trusting people generally. The urge to go through your partner's phone or monitor their Facebook often stems from jealousy, insecurity or possessiveness. These things erode trust and will quickly destroy a relationship.

Snooping can also become addictive: if you find nothing, you'll feel relief, but it will last only a short time before you find yourself in need of another hit of reassurance. What's more, snooping is a form of stalking and a major warning sign in a relationship. If you are struggling to manage jealous feelings, it's important that you speak to a trusted adult or counsellor who can help you make sense of your feelings.

Relationship violence

Q. What should I do if a friend tells me that she was sexually assaulted?

A. Someone who has been sexually assaulted may be scared that she will be blamed, shamed or simply not believed if she speaks out. It often takes a huge amount of courage and strength to make the decision to tell someone. The fact that your friend has decided to come to you means that she really trusts you, values your opinion and believes that you are a safe person to tell. Keep in mind that your words will have a powerful impact on her. Here are three things you can say to support her:

1. 'I am so sorry this happened to you.' By saying this you are telling her that you believe her.

2. 'What happened to you is a crime.' This tells her she is not to blame and that you are going to take what happened to her seriously.
3. 'I will do whatever I can to support you.' This tells her that she is not alone.[3]

Don't assume you know how she feels, but listen to how she feels. Avoid asking questions such as 'What were you wearing?' or 'Why didn't you scream or fight back?' These questions will make her feel as though you are blaming her, even if that is not your intent.

Encourage her to speak to a trusted adult or to seek expert support from a trained sexual assault counsellor. In Australia a person can call 1800 RESPECT, a 24/7 hotline which is run by qualified sexual assault and family violence counsellors.

Finally, remember that when a friend tells you that she has been assaulted, it can be highly distressing for you, particularly if you have ever experienced violence yourself. It is important that you take care of yourself and that you talk to a trusted adult; you may also want to debrief with a sexual violence counsellor, too.

Sexual assault myths and facts[4]
Myth: **Most sexual assaults are committed by strangers.**
Fact: When someone is sexually assaulted, in most cases it's by someone they already know such as a family member, friend, current or former partner,

or someone they go to school or work with. Only a fraction of sexual assaults are committed by strangers and an attack by a stranger in a dark place with a weapon — as per the cliché — is even less common.

Myth: Sexual assault is rare.
Fact: In Australia, about one in five females will experience sexual assault at some point in their lives, and women aged fifteen to twenty-four experience sexual assault at higher rates than anyone else.

Myth: Sexual assault is about uncontrollable lust.
Fact: Sexual assault is not about lust or uncontrollable hormones. It's about power, entitlement, control and humiliation.

Myth: Forced oral sex is not considered rape.
Fact: Sexual assault or rape includes any non-consensual touching or penetration of the vagina or anus with a penis, finger, tongue or any implement, or touching or penetration of the mouth by a penis or vagina.

Myth: Girls are asking for sexual assault through their dress or the way they act.
Fact: Research shows that sexual assault is not caused by how a girl looks or acts. This myth is used to excuse the actions of the person committing the assault and shift the blame and responsibility for preventing sexual violence onto women and girls.

Myth: Sexual assault always involves physical force or violence.
Fact: Sexual assault only very occasionally involves physical force or violence. Very often the person committing the assault will rely on psychological factors instead, such as intimidation, pressure, coercion, control or fear.

Myth: Sex offenders are easy to spot.
Fact: Sex offenders come from every class, culture, race, religion and community. They are not confined to any particular age group, social group or profession.

Myth: Girls lie and tell police they were sexually assaulted because they feel guilty or regretful about having sex.
Fact: Under-reporting, not false reporting, is the biggest issue. About 85 per cent of victims don't report sexual assault to the police.

Myth: Boys can't be sexually assaulted.
Fact: While most sexual violence is committed against women and girls, anyone can experience sexual assault.

Myth: Sexual assault would never happen to someone like me.
Fact: One reason victims sometimes feel shame is because they believe that sexual violence only happens to a certain type of person and that those people are

partly to blame. This is not true. Sexual assault can happen to anyone regardless of class, age, culture or appearance. No person ever wants to be sexually assaulted and no person is ever to blame for sexual violence they experience.

Q. If a girl really didn't want to be in a toxic or controlling relationship, why wouldn't she just walk away?

A. There are many reasons why it can be hard for a girl to seek help or leave a relationship that isn't respectful. She may feel shame or embarrassment for asking for help or fear that people will blame her for being in the situation in the first place. She may still care for her partner and believe that the disrespectful behaviour will change. Her partner may have manipulated her into believing that the disrespectful behaviour is her fault or that no-one else will care about it. She might fear what will happen to herself, her partner or others if the relationship ends, especially if her partner has ever made threats.

Having little support from others can also make someone more likely to stay in a disrespectful relationship. Abusive individuals know this and so will often try to isolate their partners from friends and family members, as a way of cutting off support and maintaining control.

As you can see, there are all sorts of reasons why it might be difficult for a person to seek help or leave the relationship. The idea that it is easy for a person to just walk away from a toxic relationship is just one of many myths about unhealthy relationships.

Relationship violence myths and facts

Myth: Relationship violence only affects adult couples.
Fact: Relationship violence does not only affect adults or people who live together, as the term 'domestic' violence implies. It can affect anyone regardless of their age, marital status or living status. Relationship violence in teen relationships is real and just as serious as it is for any other age group.

Myth: Relationship violence does not affect many people.
Fact: Relationship violence is still the most common form of assault in Australia, and more than one in three females will experience physical or sexual violence after the age of fifteen.

Myth: Alcohol causes relationship violence.
Fact: Sometimes alcohol can make relationship violence worse, but it is not the underlying cause.

Myth: Relationship violence only occurs in poor, uneducated or minority communities.
Fact: Relationship violence occurs among all cultures and communities regardless of race, religion, age, education level or social and economic status.

Myth: People are violent in their relationships because of stress.
Fact: There is no excuse for relationship violence, and the majority of people who get stressed do not make the decision to be violent.

Myth: Most males are violent. It's in their nature.
Fact: Violence is learnt behaviour. Most boys and men are not violent at all.

Myth: The victim is responsible for the violence because she provokes it.
Fact: People who commit violence often use this myth to try to excuse their actions. But there is no excuse for violence, ever.

Myth: Relationship violence is a 'loss of control'.
Fact: Abusers' actions are very deliberate, and they choose when and where they will explode — for example, when there are no witnesses around.

If any of this material brings up issues for you, talk to an adult you trust — such as a teacher or school counsellor — as soon as possible. Or you can call one of the hotlines listed at the back of the book and speak to a counsellor, anonymously if you prefer. Remember, you have the right to be treated with dignity and respect.

Relationship Q&A

Disagreements, arguments and break-ups

Q. I've been with my boyfriend for four months but now I can't decide whether I want to stay with him. How do I know whether to stay and what is the best way to break up with someone?

A. How to go about a break-up:

1. Get the situation clear in your head. If you are in two minds about whether to break up with someone, ask yourself these questions and decide what is going to be best for you:

- Do you feel less attracted to them than before?
- Do you find that you don't enjoy spending time with them as much as before?
- Do you no longer feel the same way as they do or want the same things any more?
- Do you live too far away from them?
- Do you feel unable to be yourself when you're with them?
- Are you more sad than happy when you're with them?
- Do you feel that you want to spend more time by yourself?
- Do you feel that things are moving too quickly or getting too serious?
- Are your boundaries being pushed or crossed?

- Are they emotionally unavailable or unsupportive?
- Do they fail to make you feel appreciated?
- Do you share few interests with them?

2. Go in with a plan. Once you've made the decision to break up with someone, work out what you want to say and what boundaries you hope to establish by the end of the conversation, including how much contact you are willing to have with them from now on. If necessary, write down what you want to say. Focus on why you want to end the relationship rather than blaming them.

3. Choose an appropriate location. If you've only been out once or twice and are not yet a couple, it's OK to tell someone by text message or email that you don't want to see them again. But if your relationship has gone on longer than that, a face-to-face break-up is in order (an important exception is if the person has ever used or threatened violence against you or made you feel unsafe). Choose a location where you will have some privacy and where the other person will not be forced to put on a brave face to friends immediately after. For example, breaking up with someone at a party is not a good idea, because even if you do it in private, they will be forced to socialise or leave the party, which doesn't give them a lot of space to process the break-up. Going for a walk or choosing a neutral place, such as a quiet coffee shop, is a good idea. Wherever you go, make sure you have a way of getting home by yourself.

4. Be gentle but firm. You don't need to go into every little detail, and try not to assign blame, but be clear that the relationship is no longer working for you and that you want to break up. Avoid the expression 'I think we should see other people'. Instead just be upfront and say, 'I've thought about this long and hard, and I've decided it's best that we break up.' If the relationship lasted a significant amount of time, or if you think that there are things it would be helpful for the other person to hear, give your reasons. After all, when we don't understand the reasons behind a break-up it can be hard to move on. Avoid making fickle criticisms about the other person. (Hey, you might not like someone's Dr Who obsession, but who's to say that the next girl won't?) If someone tries to debate the reasons for the break-up, tell them that you are sorry they're hurting, but you have made your decision and your decision is final.

5. Establish some new boundaries. Tell your ex what (if any) level of contact you are prepared to continue to have. Don't assume that the person will know to stop calling or texting you. If you want to set a time frame on when you are willing to see your ex next, do so. Get your ex to verbally agree to it. For example, you could say, 'I think it's best if we don't contact or see each other for at least a month.' This might sound tough, but it's important that you communicate your expectations. If you go to the same school, work together, or hang out in the same social group, you'll need to come up with a plan for dealing with this, too. This step is particularly important if you have tried to end things before and your words have been ignored.

You may want to stay friends after the break-up, but there is no rule that says you have to. If you do decide to remain friends, it's best to give it some time and let the dust settle. Avoid the temptation to hook up with an ex. This is messy business and almost always creates complications that stop one or both of you from moving on. It can feel comfortable, but it only draws out the painful process of ending a relationship, so set a firm boundary around physical intimacy.

6. Honour what you had. The ending of a relationship doesn't erase the imprint that you left on each other, the good times that you shared or the lessons you both learnt. Even if you cannot be friends, don't trash your ex or relationship to others. You'll be happier in the long run if you can let go of the bad stuff while remembering some of the good times.

You can tell a lot about a guy by how he speaks about his exes. If he is angry or bitter about one ex, there could be valid reasons. But if he is angry and bitter about all of them, the common factor is probably him. Also, if a guy uses sexist language — such as 'bitch' or 'slut' — when talking about his exes, it's a warning sign that he doesn't really respect girls (and there is no reason to assume he won't talk about you like that one day). By contrast, if your new guy talks about his exes with respect, this is a green light.

Q. My boyfriend and I seem to argue a lot. Does this mean we are doomed?

A. All couples argue to some degree and it is totally normal. But *how* you argue, the things you argue about, and the frequency, duration and intensity of your arguments matter. If you ever feel scared or unsafe, or if fighting ever becomes emotionally abusive or physical, then this is a serious problem. Likewise, if you are fighting because there is a lack of trust or respect in the relationship, you will need to address those issues.

Ask yourself what sorts of things you argue about. Are they serious things relating to your core values, such as jealousy, infidelity or pressure to have sex? Or do you argue about preferences or trivial things, such as which TV show to watch? How long do your arguments tend to last? And do you resolve arguments well?

It may sound strange, but learning to fight fair is an important skill in a relationship. Calm discussion is always better than heated argument, so you might want to review the 10 Steps to Conflict Resolution in this chapter. Here are some additional tips for fighting fair:

- Pick your battles. Not every little thing is worth arguing about. Only raise an issue because you want to seek a resolution, not just to pick a fight.
- Maintain control of your voice and actions. Don't yell or swear, and check your aggression levels.
- Avoid character assassinations. This means no name-calling or belittling of the other person. Also have a 'no low blows' rule. Don't attack someone based on things that are outside their control — for example, 'No wonder your father left you and your mother. You're such a nightmare to be around!'
- Avoid exaggerations. Try not to use words such as 'always' and 'never'.
- Avoid comparing your partner to other people, especially your previous partners, and don't compare your relationship to other people's relationships.
- Avoid making threats — for example, don't threaten to break up if you don't mean it.
- Don't involve other people's opinions — for example, 'Well, my friend Sophie agrees with me. She says that it's not normal for you to spend so much time on the computer.'
- Avoid the use of power plays such as emotional blackmail ('if you really loved me, then you'd …'), point scoring ('that's the

fourth time we've done what you wanted. We've only done what I wanted twice'), the silent treatment, sulking, guilt tripping ('my last boyfriend would always pay for that sort of thing') or playing the martyr ('it doesn't matter, anyway. I'm used to being disappointed').

- If things get too heated, have a timeout. It takes most people at least half an hour for their physiology — including heart rate, breathing and blood pressure — to return to normal after a heated exchange.
- Say sorry when you are wrong, and mean it.
- Give your partner the option to retreat with dignity or change their mind.
- If the issue is likely to come up again in the future, it's better to sort it out while you are talking about it and make a plan for how you will deal with it when it comes up again.
- Fights need a time limit on them. Even if you just agree to a truce, don't allow a fight to go on for more than half an hour.
- If the matter is trivial, and the relationship is worth having, then always be willing to fix the problem. You're on the same team.

Q. My boyfriend isn't like he used to be. He's more negative, and it's bringing me down. I'm worried that

if I break it off, he might get worse. He often tells me I'm the only good thing in his life. What should I do?

A. Sometimes when we care about someone who is going through a tough time or is feeling depressed, we can end up putting their needs ahead of our own. This is especially true when we are worried that our need to take a break from the relationship might cause our partner extra pain or anxiety. Sometimes we feel so responsible about another person's happiness that we stay in a relationship that makes us feel unhappy, just to avoid hurting the person's feelings.

But the reality is that guilt is never a good reason to stay with a person. You will end up feeling hostile and resentful towards your boyfriend. And he will pick up on the fact that you are not happy, which will only further contribute to his feelings of guilt, frustration and depression. In other words, you're not doing you or your boyfriend any favours by staying with him if you are no longer happy.

It might be hard to hear this, but you need to put aside his feelings and needs for one minute and concentrate on your own. It's not selfish to look after your own needs. Are you happy? Are you having fun? Do you feel enriched by the relationship? Or are you staying with your boyfriend because you need to be needed or you fear what will happen to his wellbeing if you break up with him? If this is the case, then the relationship does not sound all that fulfilling or satisfying.

So what do you do about it? Get some emotional distance. Talk to a trusted adult to help you process some of your own emotions about what is going on.

Remember that you are not a trained counsellor and are not responsible for someone else's psychological wellbeing. If your boyfriend is feeling down all the time, he may be depressed and in need of professional help. The best thing you can do is encourage him to get professional support and talk to an adult that you trust.

Note: if ever a person threatens to hurt themselves, don't ignore it. Seek help from an adult immediately.

Q. I just broke up with my boyfriend. A lot of his stuff is still at my house and I still have lots of presents he gave me. Looking at them makes me sad. What should I do with this stuff?

A. Start by going through your home and packing any objects that belong to him into a box. Be thorough, because you don't want to set off the emotional rollercoaster by finding a forgotten pair of sunglasses of his in a few weeks time. If you've agreed not to see each other for a set period, you might want to get a mutual friend to drop off this stuff to your ex-boyfriend. If the relationship ended badly and you're mad at him, don't throw out or destroy any of his property out of revenge. You'll only feel bad about this later. Keep it classy, lady, and you'll feel better about yourself down the track.

My personal rule is that it's OK to keep any presents that are given in a relationship, with the possible exception of really expensive gifts, jewellery that was a family heirloom or an engagement ring. But if looking at the stuff your ex gave you makes you feel sad, you could put it in a box and store it away for later. If you want to get rid of it, you could consider giving it to charity.

Q. I became friends with my ex's friends when we were together. Can I still be friends with them even though I broke up with my ex?
A. The issue of friends is a lot trickier. The most important thing is that you don't make mutual friends take sides or bad-mouth your ex to them. This will only alienate them. If you have agreed not to see your ex for a while, you may need to allow some time before hanging out with his friends as a group, but be sure to let them know that you value their friendship and the time you have spent with them. Sometimes friends can feel as though you have 'dropped' them if you suddenly cut off all contact. You might want to organise one-on-one catch-ups with them, but be sure to set a 'no relationship talk' rule. Hopefully, when the time is right, you'll be able to continue to hang out with them as a group.

Q. I just broke up with my partner. How long should I wait until I date again?
A. There is no set period of time that it takes to be ready to date again. Some people move on from relationships

quickly, especially if they had already processed a lot of the feelings by the time it came to ending the relationship, while others can take a lot longer. What matters is that you feel ready and comfortable to move on. If you are still grieving or are still in love with your ex and are simply looking for a distraction, you may end up hurting someone if you jump into anything too soon (hello, rebound territory!). Before dating someone new, try to reflect on the relationship that has just ended. Why did it end? What have you learnt from it? What would you do differently in a new relationship? All relationships teach us something, and relationships that end help us to work out what we really want in a partner.

So that's it from us. Take a deep breath, hold your head high and off you go! Adventure awaits!

RESOURCES

Useful websites, organisations and books

Enlighten Education
Gifts for you:

FREE iPhone app, The Butterfly Effect: Get your daily dose of awesome, delivered straight to your iPhone.

- Affirmation — messages to boost self-esteem and body image.
- Inspiration — wise words from amazing women.
- Information — web links to info every girl needs to know.

FREE wallpapers for your phone: Make your phone not just pretty but also positive, with one of Enlighten's gorgeous posters as your wallpaper.

To download the free iPhone app and wallpapers, go to: www.enlighteneducation.com/shop

Enlighten Education on Facebook:
www.facebook.com
- 'Like' the Enlighten Education page on Facebook to join a community of thousands of other Amazon girls and women who want to make a difference!

Enlighten Education on Instagram:
#enlighteneducation
- Follow Enlighten Education!

Enlighten Education company website:
www.enlighteneducation.com
- Delivers in-school workshops for girls on self-esteem, body image, managing friendships, personal safety and career pathways.

The Butterfly Effect:
www.enlighteneducation.edublogs.org
- Danni's blog, with weekly posts on hot topics related to girls.

Positive self-esteem and body image
Websites
American sites providing media literacy skills needed to combat unhelpful media messages about beauty and body image:

About-Face: www.about-face.org
Adios Barbie: www.adiosbarbie.com
AnyBody: www.any-body.org
Love Your Body NOW Foundation:
http://loveyourbody.nowfoundation.org
My Pop Studio: www.mypopstudio.com

Other useful websites
Girlpower Retouch:
http://demo.fb.se/e/girlpower/retouch
- A site that shows how easy it is to distort the images we see in magazines and change someone's appearance.

Jean Kilbourne: www.jeankilbourne.com
- Writer and documentary maker who explores the way women and girls are portrayed in advertising.

Beautiful Women Project:
www.beautifulwomenproject.net
- American art project celebrating diversity and real, everyday beauty.

Girlguiding UK: www.girlguiding.org.uk
- The section 'Girls Shout Out' has some particularly interesting reports on teenage mental health, active citizenship and pressures of growing up.

Australian Council on Children and the Media: http://childrenandmedia.org.au
- Australian organisation with a particular interest in developing media literacy in young people.

Books
The Girl with the Butterfly Tattoo, Dannielle Miller, Random House, 2012.
Girl Stuff: Your Full-on Guide to the Teen Years, Kaz Cooke, Penguin, 2007.
Body Talk: A Power Guide for Girls, Elizabeth Reid Boyd and Abigail Bray, Hodder Headline, 2005.
The Girlosophy series, Anthea Paul, Allen and Unwin.
The Girlforce series, Nikki Goldstein, ABC Books.

Friendship
Website
Bullying. No Way!: http://bullyingnoway.gov.au
- Australian site that aims to develop and share frameworks for schools that work in eliminating bullying.

Book

Respect: A Girl's Guide to Getting Respect and Dealing When Your Line is Crossed, Courtney Macavinta and Andrea Vander Pluym, Free Spirit Publishing, 2005.

Teen girls in crisis
Specialist

Our psychologist advisor Jacqui Manning (aka the Friendly Psychologist):
www.thefriendlypsychologist.com.au

Websites

NSW Rape Crisis Centre: www.nswrapecrisis.com.au
- Comprehensive information about sexual assault.

National Children's and Youth Law Centre:
www.ncylc.org.au
- Offers a complete breakdown of laws that affect young people by State and Territory. People under eighteen can access free legal advice through their lawmail service.

Beyondblue: www.beyondblue.org.au
- Australian website on depression.

Black Dog Institute: www.blackdoginstitute.org.au
- Australian website on depression.

National Prescribing Service: www.nps.org.au
- Consumer advice on medications, funded by the Australian Government Department of Health and Ageing.

Reach Out: www.reachout.com.au
- Advice targeted to young people, on their mental health and wellbeing.

Youth Beyondblue: www.youthbeyondblue.com
- Australian website about young people and depression.

The Butterfly Foundation: http://thebutterflyfoundation.org.au
- Supports Australians with eating disorders.

Suicide Prevention: http://suicidepreventionaust.org
- Public health advocates in suicide and self-harm prevention.

Book
It Will Get Better: Finding Your Way Through Teen Issues, Melinda Hutchings, Allen and Unwin, 2010.

Feminism
Website
Miss Representation: www.missrepresentation.org
- Media literacy with a gender focus.

Books
Your Skirt's Too Short: Sex, Power, Choice, Emily Maguire, Text Publishing, 2010.

Full Frontal Feminism: A Young Woman's Guide to Why Feminism Matters, Jessica Valenti, Seal Press, 2007.

Sexuality and health
Websites
Sexual Health and Family Planning Australia: www.shfpa.org.au
- Comprehensive information on sexual health, including puberty, contraception, etc.

Scarleteen: www.scarleteen.com
- Inclusive, comprehensive and smart sexuality information and help for teens.

Sex, Etc.: http://sexetc.org
- Teen-to-teen sex education.

The Consensual Project: www.theconsensualproject.com
- Understanding consent and communication.

It Gets Better Project: www.itgetsbetter.org
- Support and discussion on issues affecting GLBT youth.

Books

Puberty Girl, Shushann Movsessian, Allen and Unwin, 2004.

My Little Red Book, Rachel Kauder Nalebuff, Twelve, 2010.

Queer: The Ultimate LGBT Guide for Teens, Kathy Belge and Marke Bieschke, Zest Books, 2011.

The Purity Myth: How America's Obsession with Virginity is Hurting Young Women, Jessica Valenti, Seal Press, 2009.

He's a Stud, She's a Slut and 49 Other Double Standards Every Woman Should Know, Jessica Valenti, Seal Press, 2008.

The First Time: True Tales of Virginity Lost and Found, Kate Munro, Icon Books, 2011.

Yes Means Yes: Visions of Female Sexual Power and a World Without Rape, Jaclyn Friedman and Jessica Valenti, Seal Press, 2008.

QLBTQ*: The Survival Guide for Queer and Questioning Teens, Kelly Huegel, Free Spirit Publishing, 2003.

Get help NOW!

National Sexual Assault, Domestic and Family Violence Counselling Service: 1800 RESPECT or 1800 737 732

- 24/7 counselling service for individuals who have experienced sexual, family or relationship violence, and their supporters.

Lifeline: 13 11 14

- 24/7 crisis hotline.

Kids Helpline: 1800 55 1800

- 24/7 counselling helpline for children and young people.

ENDNOTES

Chapter 1: Planet Romance — what to pack
1. Andrew P. Smiler, *Challenging Casanova*, Jossey-Bass, San Francisco, 2012, pp. 30, 56, 58.
2. ibid., p. 183.
3. This exercise on relationship value setting was provided by psychologist Jacqui Manning.

Chapter 3: Crushing dilemmas: what happens when the feelings are not mutual?
1. 'Twenty-two Kisses, Four Relationships and Five Broken Hearts: What It Takes to Find Mr Right', *Daily Mail*, www.dailymail.co.uk/news/article-1367082/Twenty-kisses-relationships-broken-hearts-What-takes-Mr-Right.html, 17 March 2011.
2. Chiara Atik, 'How to Find "The One": The Dating Theory That Could (No Joke!) Change Your Life', How About We, www.howaboutwe.com/date-report/2080-how-to-find-the-one-the-dating-theory-that-could-no-joke-change-your-life/#, 17 November 2011.
3. OWN, 'Oprah's Life Lesson from Maya Angelou: "When People Show You Who They Are, Believe Them"', *The Huffington Post*, www.huffingtonpost.com/2013/03/14/oprah-life-lesson-maya-angelou_n_2869235.html, 14 March 2013.
4. This advice on how to let someone down gently if they have a crush on you was provided by psychologist Jacqui Manning.

5   Interview with Chloe Angyal via email, 20 September 2012.

Chapter 4: Deal makers and deal breakers
1   This quote comes from a speech given by Michelle Obama on 25 May 2011 at Oxford University. See: www.whitehouse.gov/the-press-office/2011/05/25/remarks-first-lady-event-elizabeth-garrett-anderson-students.
2   Adapted from the Healthy Relationships Checklist, LEAP (Look to End Abuse Permanently), www.leapsf.org/html/healthy_relationships_checklist.shtml.

Chapter 5: So you're dating! Now what?
1   This advice on how to reassert your boundaries in a relationship was provided by psychologist Jacqui Manning.

Chapter 7: Healing heartbreak
1   Elizabeth Gilbert, *Eat, Pray, Love*, Penguin Books, New York, 2007.
2   Yashar Ali, 'Why He Gets Over a Breakup Faster than You Do', *The Huffington Post*, www.huffingtonpost.com/yashar-hedayat/breakup_b_1724395.html?ncid=edlinkusaolp00000003, 2 August 2012.
3   Brené Brown, *The Gifts of Imperfection: Let Go of Who You Think You're Supposed to Be and Embrace Who You Are*, Hazelden, Center City, Minnesota, 2010, pp. 72–73.
4   This visualisation exercise is based on psychologist Karyn Hall's coping strategies for people who are especially sensitive to being criticised by others.
5   Brené Brown, *The Gifts of Imperfection: Let Go of Who You Think You're Supposed to Be and Embrace Who You Are*, Hazelden, Center City, Minnesota, 2010, p. 11. On pp. 10–11, Brown discusses why it's important to make careful choices about whom you turn to for compassion.
6   Terri St Cloud, www.bonesigharts.com.

7   This advice on the steps to forgiveness was provided by psychologist Jacqui Manning.

Chapter 8: Single? In a relationship? Who cares? I'm awesome!

1   Samara O'Shea, 'The Grass is Rarely (Almost Never) Greener', *The Huffington Post*, www.huffingtonpost.com/samara-oshea/the-grass-is-rarely-almos_b_96981.html, 16 April 2008.
2   Rebecca Mead, 'Princess for a Day', *The Guardian*, www.guardian.co.uk/lifeandstyle/2010/aug/07/weddings-industry-commercial-giles-fraser, 6 August 2010.
3   William Marston is quoted in Noah Berlatsky, 'Toward a More Expansive Definition of "Princess"', *The Atlantic*, www.theatlantic.com/sexes/archive/2013/05/toward-a-more-expansive-definition-of-princess/276088/, 21 May 2013.
4   Robert Munsch, illustrated by Michael Martchenko, *The Paper Bag Princess*, Scholastic Press, Sydney, 2007.
5   This figure comes from Erna Paris, 'Witchcraze: A New History of the European Witch Hunts', *The Globe and Mail*, 30 July 1994, C.13.
6   Emily Maguire, *Your Skirt's Too Short: Sex, Power, Choice*, Text Publishing, Melbourne, 2010, p. 15.
7   One Thousand Single Days, 'About the Author', http://onethousandsingledays.com/what-does-one-thousand-days-even-mean-2/.
8   Barbara Fredrickson is quoted in Emily Esfahani Smith, 'There's No Such Thing as Everlasting Love (According to Science)', *The Atlantic*, www.theatlantic.com/sexes/archive/2013/01/theres-no-such-thing-as-everlasting-love-according-to-science/267199/, 24 January 2013. The book in which she writes about her research is *Love 2.0: How Our Supreme Emotion Affects Everything We Feel, Think, Do, and Become*, Hudson Street Press, New York, 2013.
9   These statistics come from 'Australian Census: One in Ten Live Alone, but That Doesn't Mean They're Lonely', The Conversation, http://theconversation.edu.au/australian-

census-one-in-ten-live-alone-but-that-doesnt-mean-theyre-lonely-7674, 22 June 2012.

Chapter 9: Relationship Q&A

1 Based on Gary Chapman, *The Five Love Languages of Teenagers*, Northfield Publishing, Chicago, 2010.
2 Based on the respect rules in Courtney Macavinta and Andrea Vander Pluym, *Respect: A Girl's Guide to Getting Respect and Dealing When Your Line is Crossed*, Free Spirit Publishing, Minneapolis, 2005.
3 Adapted from NSW Rape Crisis Centre, www.nswrapecrisis.com.au.
4 These are adapted from NSW Rape Crisis Centre factsheets: 'Sexual Assault: The Law and Statistics', www.nswrapecrisis.com.au/Portals/0/PDF/Sexual%20Assault%20The%20Law%20and%20Statistics.pdf; 'Sexual Assault: Myths and Facts', www.nswrapecrisis.com.au/Portals/0/PDF/Sexual%20Assault%20Myths%20and%20Facts.pdf; 'Common Impacts of Sexual Assault', www.nswrapecrisis.com.au/Portals/0/PDF/Common%20Impacts%20of%20Sexual%20Assault.pdf; 'Perpetrator Tactics', www.nswrapecrisis.com.au/Portals/0/Information%20Sheets/images/Factsheets/Perpetrator%20Tactics%20-%20Jun%202012.pdf.

ACKNOWLEDGMENTS

by Danni

I am sincerely and forever grateful for the following people.

At Enlighten Education:
All the teenage girls I have worked with. You shine so brightly that at times I am almost blinded by your magnificence. Love, Light and Laughter to you all.

The schools that allow me the privilege of working with their girls.

Francesca Kaoutal, my Yellow Brick Road partner who always says 'yes' and always offers me the warmest, wisest advice. You, my darling Franster, are the family I chose.

Storm Greenhill-Brown, Sam Corfield, Nikki Davis, Lauren Muscat and Meredith Tourell — my Enlighten Amazons who have not only shared the dream but have helped it grow larger and more vivid. Thank you, also, Christine Elias — my tireless right-hand gal who makes Enlighten HQ the most positive and productive place to work. Thanks, too, to Tessa Steen, who seemingly never tires of writing out all the evaluations we receive from the girls we work with.

In my writing:
My publisher at HarperCollins, Lisa Berryman. Your support and enthusiasm for this project, and for my work in general, has been truly a gift. A gift wrapped in sparkly paper with a shiny satin ribbon tied beautifully on top. I wish to also acknowledge the efficient and always delightful Kate Burnitt, for all her support in collating edits.

Vanessa Mickan, my divine editor, who has made this whole writing process such an absolute joy. V — you are my literary angel. Still. Always.

My writing partner, Nina Funnell. Nina, I am honoured to be your 'Dumbledore' and am frequently enchanted by your own magic and bravery. It has been such fun twirling words, and worrying about cupcakes, with you.

The incredible women and specialists who allowed me to interview them for this book. It is richer for your contributions. I wish to particularly acknowledge the assistance offered by psychologist Jacqui Manning and my 'feminist crush' Emily Maguire.

All the teenage girls I interviewed — and a special shoutout to my darlings Ella, Jemma, Melanie, Jacqueline and Madison. You are incredible young women with such interesting insights into the world. I hear you.

In my life:
My children, Teyah and Kye, for not only accepting my work but sharing my passion for it, too. You are such loving, amusing, top-shelf children. I am so proud and privileged to do life with you both.

My special Jazmine Brightwell. We don't need a label to know that what we have is real. You will always be in my heart, too, Jazzy.

My Facebook friends — you are more than mere cyber acquaintances. I 'like' being connected to a community that is diverse, questioning and so often highly amusing.

My fabulous housemate Jess. You have been a breath of fresh air and a brilliant *Game of Thrones* partner.

All my closest friends, in particular my soul sisters — Sarah (aka Sassy Pants), Brooke-the-Bad-Arse-Christian, Sonia, Jane, Mel and Sharon. And my soul brother Aaron. xxx

by Nina

I am sincerely thankful to all the people who have worked on getting this project across the line. It's been an incredible journey! Thank you to Lisa Berryman at HarperCollins for all your amazing effort. You have truly driven the project from the beginning. I'd also like to acknowledge and thank Vanessa Mickan and

Kate Burnitt, our wonderful editors who have put in countless hours of work.

A special thank you to all the courageous women and girls who have been so generous in adding their voices to the book, especially Jacqui Manning, Stella Young, Chloe Angyal, Nikki Davis and the divine Ms Lily Edelstein. All of you women inspire me. And of course, last but not least, a massive thank you to my wonderful co-conspirator and partner in crime, Danni. Without your vision and initiative this project would never have taken shape.

In my personal life, I would also like to thank a number of people who have encouraged and supported me over the years. A huge thank you to Catharine Lumby and Karen Willis, two amazing Amazon women who have provided me with countless hours of counsel and support. Both of you have taught and inspired me and I am forever grateful for all that I have learnt from you. In your separate ways, you both make the world a better place for women and girls.

Thank you to all the strong, feminist women in my life. You have been my teachers, mentors and friends. I value and adore all of you.

Finally, I must thank the people who have taught me most about love. Thank you to my mum, dad and brother, Alister. You have encouraged me at every turn and I love you all. Most of all, thank you to my darling partner, Jeb. Your wisdom and wit have made every day with you an exciting adventure. You have also been a pillar of support while writing this book and I am eternally grateful for your patience, encouragement and generosity of spirit! Words cannot describe how lucky I am to have you.

Printed in Australia
AUHW02081211021
354047AU00009B/307

9 780732 296469